THAT BOWLING ALLEY
ON THE TIBER

That Bowling Alley on the Tiber

TALES OF A DIRECTOR

Michelangelo Antonioni

Translated from the Italian by
William Arrowsmith

New York   Oxford
OXFORD UNIVERSITY PRESS
1986

Oxford University Press

Oxford   New York   Toronto
Delhi   Bombay   Calcutta   Madras   Karachi
Petaling Jaya   Singapore   Hong Kong   Tokyo
Nairobi   Dar es Salaam   Cape Town
Melbourne   Auckland

and associated companies in
Beirut   Berlin   Ibadan   Nicosia

Library of Congress Cataloging in Publication Data
Antonioni, Michelangelo.
That bowling alley on the Tiber.
Translation of: Quel bowling sul Tevere.
I. Title.
PQ4861.N823Q813   1985   853'.914   85-11458
ISBN 0-19-503676-X

Printing (last digit): 9 8 7 6 5 4 3 2 1

Printed in the United States of America

Contents

Translator's Preface

Dark things are drawn to brighter,
bodies thin away in a flowing
of colors, colors in musics. So
disappearance is the greatest adventure.
MONTALE, "Portami il girasole . . ."

Ostensibly these thirty-three "sketches," "story-ideas," or "narrative nuclei" are intended to provide Antonioni's reader (reasonably assumed to be a spectator too) with an invitation to explore the director's workshop, his modes of observation, and the genesis of his films. "I'm a director who writes, not a writer." Antonioni's disclaimer is designed, not to ask the reader's indulgence (of which he has, in any case, no need), but to stress the visual and, above all, visually kinetic habits of observation and narration at work in the films. We encounter not merely a transcription of narrative to cinematic terms, as when "the eye pans," or dawn "begins its fade-in," or an action "seems out of sync" with the spoken words, or we hear a voice "off-screen," but rather the verbalization of pre-cinematic material in terms of its kinetic potential. Antonioni's tentative term for these sketches—which have no established generic definition—is "nucleus," "matrix," or "embryo." The stress falls on the interior activity, the inward dynamic, whether conceived physically or biologically, of an image or a situation. The nucleus has a quantum of unknown, because unrealized, energy capable like a charged particle of combining with other material, then taking on mass and finally visible form. Or, like an embryo, a capacity for maturing and ripening, for revealing hidden genetic properties in a complex organism whose eventual nature cannot be predicted. The nucleus and embryo share what the ancient philosophers called entelechy: an immanent power of actualization, an inward propensity for self-revelation, or purposive essence. The energy of the nucleus may be dormant, abeyant, or latent, but it is *there*—a miniature cinematic potentiality awaiting that intervention by director and camera that will thrust it toward full visual and kinetic actualization.

Unlike painting, cinema is *all* movement, an image of movement itself. At its expressive best, it is the ideal medium for narrating the experience of life as current or flux—the flow of feelings before they achieve articulation in word or action, the sensation of process and change, of growing, ripening, aging, shifts of perspective, the subtler changes in social or personal weather. Painting has the power to express the timeless moment when foreground and background, transient and eternal, seem to merge. But in film that same moment is revealed by process, by an unscrolling epiphany, as a pack of gathering particulars might suddenly precipitate their unity in a summative cadence. Thus in Antonioni's exquisite early documentary *N.U.*, or *Netezza urbana*, the sequence of blue-bloused streetcleaners at work with their brooms in the dawn light precipitates an image of all Rome, its beauty and ugliness fused at that precise metaphysical moment which transforms a documentary into visual poetry. Hence, too, the extraordinary power and intensity of the final shots of the feature films—the beautifully crafted montage of *Eclipse*, the closing sequence and "dissolve" of *Blow-Up*, the breathtaking coda of *The Passenger*, and *Identification of a Woman*—in which Antonioni proves himself the supreme living master of cinematic cadence.

But to grasp the nature of these nuclei fully, it is important to understand that kinetic quality that makes film so expressively different from painting. In Antonioni's words:

Seeing is for us [film directors] a necessity. For the painter too the problem is seeing. But whereas for the painter it is a matter of

revealing a static reality, or a rhythm perhaps but a rhythm that
is enclosed in the sign, the director's problem is that of embracing
a reality that ripens and consumes itself, and to set forth this movement, this reaching a point and then advancing, as fresh perception.
Film is not image: landscape, posture, gesture. But rather an in-
dissoluble whole extended over a duration of its own that saturates
it and determines its very essence.

And again, with a different but no less crucial emphasis, and
with profound bearing on the ultimate aspiration of these nuclei:

> We know that underneath the revealed image there is another that
> is more faithful to reality, and beneath this still another, and again
> another under this last. And on up to that true image of that
> absolute, mysterious reality that nobody will ever see. Or perhaps
> up to the point at which every image, every reality, decomposes.
> Abstract film would in this way have its own reason for existing.

In the seeded nucleus the film germinates; the germ sprouts,
grows, ramifies. First as script, then as finished screenplay (in
whose preparation the director usually seeks sympathetic but
critical collaborators in order to subject a private vision to the
scrutiny of others). Then comes the crucial stage of shooting, in
which the scenario is tested—revised, cut, amplified, qualified—
by a *praxis* that involves the decisively active participation of the
camera—"the third who walks always beside you," it might be
called—of the actors, the crew, the weather, the light. It is at
this stage that improvisation enters—that adventitious reality
for which Antonioni always leaves room while shooting, the source,
he says, of some of his best *trouvailles*. And finally there is that
exhausting but lapidary task of editing the film. Of ensuring that
the finished work adequately expresses the director's governing
vision, above all his declared ambition to respect the ultimate
mystery, that reality that recedes from his grasp just as it comes
into focus. Of imposing an order large enough to indicate the
disorder it cannot reveal but only suggest—the problematic so-
lution that will in turn provoke the next film, perhaps nudging
one of those nuclei into sudden life.

Antonioni's approach here is that of "working backwards from a series of images to a state of affairs." The images are not merely observed oddities, but rather formidable oddities that have excited the observer's conscious attention—either because they are related to the activity of his own unconscious, where something unknown, some disturbance of buried feeling or association, of personal or genetic memory, is stirring in the depths. Or it may be a flash of clarity, the shock of recognition at the apparition of some thought or intuition momentarily stabbing into his darkness. The nucleus, that is, may have its source either in some obsessive or inexplicably recurrent image or in the articulation of a visual insight troubled into thematic existence by contact, at a propitious moment, with the external world—that world of which, Antonioni, as a director who began by making documentaries, has always been a precise and passionate observer. Images of the obsessional and recurrent sort would be, I suppose, those of lights—headlights in particular—seen shining dimly underwater (like Piero's car in *Eclipse* or that of the car in the sketch "They've Murdered a Man"), through the scrim of fog or rain (as in *Identification of a Woman* and *La notte*), or against the darkness (as in "Toward the Frontier").

Later, the director will explain these images as embodying his sense of quotidian reality, but their vividness and power lie in the mystery that precedes, and supersedes, his explanation. Another example would be those mountainscapes that fill his films, erotically shaped like a woman's body, or more ruggedly as those huge barriers that at once confine but also reach out for the horizon beyond them (like those mountains that in "The Event Horizon" ring the tree-fringed plateau and its grim scenario, but at one point open out toward sea and sky). Images of the intuitional kind might be the woman's appointment book in the same sketch—the date marked in bold red caps, like a destiny scrawled in blood—or, even more striking, the manicured hand of a man daintily holding a coffee spoon stained with blood ("as though in such a situation it made more sense to mix blood than coffee") found among the human pulp scattered around the crashed plane.

These latter images are generated, not by the unconscious, but by the revealing incongruities of the modern world—its schizophrenic capacity for violence juxtaposed with the comforting civilities, the cosmetic amenities we employ to conceal our inward violence from ourselves and to screen out the intrusive terror of reality as well as the danger and precariousness of existence. Whether generated by the unconscious or active poetic perception, both kinds of image shed light upon the director's lifelong habit of excavating what he sees and feels in order to bring to light an otherwise buried reality. The archaeological metaphor is his own:

My films are always works of searching. I don't consider myself a director who has already mastered his profession, but one who is continuing his search and studying his contemporaries. I'm looking (perhaps in every film) for the traces of feeling in men, and of course in women too, in a world where those traces have been buried to make way for sentiments of convenience and appearance: a world where feelings have been "public-relationized." My work is like digging, it's archaeological research among the arid material of our times. That's how I started my first film, and that's what I'm still doing . . .*

To continue the metaphor, these nuclei would represent the objects—fragments of feeling, shards of insight—uncovered in the course of a "dig." Then, brought to light, they are hefted by the imagination, examined, and tentatively assigned a place in the larger forms which they seem to suggest and fit. But the excavator's purpose is to discover, out of this detritus, out of his own buried feelings and past, who he is here and now, who he might be. The director makes films because his art is his chosen means of coming to know, of realizing himself. "A director," says An-

* This statement comes from an interview—one of the most revealing Antonioni has ever made—entitled "Let's talk about *Zabriskie Point*," published in *Esquire* (August 1970).

tonioni in the same place, "does nothing but search for himself in his films. They are documents not of a finished thought but of a thought in the making. Often one is asked: How is a film born? The probable answer is that it is born in the disorder that is in us all: the difficulty lies in finding the skein, in knowing how to pull the right thread from the skein . . ."

Film, in sum, as self-discovery. The point is made explicit in the schematic analogy drawn between painting and cinema in *Blow-Up*. The painter Bill stands looking at one of his own paintings on the studio floor: pastel dots, the latent trace of some figurative element looming in the dots, a pinkish-white opaque background. An abstraction of sorts. "They don't mean anything when I do them—just a mess," he says. "Afterwards I find something to hang onto—like . . . like . . . [and pointing to the figurative element] that leg. And then it sorts itself out. It adds up. It's like finding a clue in a detective story." "Once they're done," says Antonioni of his films, "I recognize my own intentions." Bill refuses to sell the painting to his photographer friend because the meaning—the meaning that is himself-in-the-making—is still incubating. Later, the photographer will come to recognize himself and his own vicarious complicity in the crime which—thanks to his collaborators, his camera and enlarger—he has discovered. The final blow-up—all that is left him—an image of his own and all human fate—that grainy corpse decomposing into the ground, is *his, his* abstraction, the means by which he presumably moves, disappearing into a fresh personal and professional horizon, a new mystery.

Like Locke in *The Passenger*, the photographer in *Blow-Up* is a man in the process of disappearing. The old self dies, moving "off the frame," so that the new self may make its appearance. For this disappearance to take place, a radical stripping must occur. Habits, conventional responses, encoded attitudes that prohibit meaningful communication with others as well as with one's own inward reality, professional equipment (when, as in *The Passenger*, it impedes the process of discovery) must be ruthlessly scrapped. It is excess baggage, the luggage of lies we all carry around with us, which confine us and render us incapable of change, of a new direction or dimension of reality. And so the film chops away at Locke's luggage—his tape recorder, his journalistic protocol of meaningless questions, his habits, his Faustian cars, even his dark glasses—leaving him culturally naked to confront his chosen destiny—the new man emerging at the very moment of dying.

This systematic *dépouillement* Antonioni, one of the great experimenters and pioneers, the greatest cinematic Modernist, has consistently and typically demanded of himself. Bored with conventional ways of story-telling and standard cinematic methods, he has tried to strip away routines that impeded his access to the reality that conventional film-making left unexpressed and to that degree, impoverished itself. After *La notte* (1960), he said:

> I believe I've managed to strip myself bare, to liberate myself from the many unnecessary formal techniques that were so common at the time. . . . So I've rid myself of much useless technical baggage, eliminating all the logical transitions, all those connective links between sequences where one sequence served as a springboard for the one that followed. The reason I did this was that I believe . . . that cinema today should be tied to the truth rather than to logic. And the truth of our daily lives is neither mechanical, conventional, nor artificial, as stories generally are, and if films are made that way, they'll show it. . . . So I think it's important for cinema to turn toward . . . ways of expression that are absolutely free, as free as painting which has reached abstraction; perhaps cinema will even construct poetry, a cinematic poem in rhyme.*

By stripping himself in this way to achieve a poetic rather than merely conventional truth, the director tends to disappear into his own work. His cinematic poetry is the inevitable consequence

---

* From a discussion that took place in March 1961, at the Centro Sperimentale di Cinematografia in Rome, and originally appeared in the Centro's journal, *Bianco e Nero*, n. 2–3 (February/March 1961).

of what Eliot (Antonioni's favorite modern poet), with less than his usual precision, called "impersonal poetry"—a poetry achieved by "a continuous extinction of personality." But for Eliot, as for Rémy de Gourmont by whom he was influenced, that disappearance was essentially a movement from the periphery toward the "crystal" or inward horizon of one's being. The aim was to work one's way beneath that suffocating carapace of received ideas and routinized feelings, the merely conditioned self that speaks in clichés and thinks in stereotypes, burrowing down to what Eliot called that "tougher self, who does not speak,/who never talks, who cannot argue." Like reality, that self constantly eludes the director's grasp; for this reason each completed film is always merely tentative, an end that turns out to be a beginning. But it is the effort, the *struggle* to transcend the self for which one no longer has any use, that finally matters. Like the poet, the director (and those characters who bear the imprint of his quest) goes as far as he can since there's no real point in heading for any horizon that does not take us to the point at which we discover just how far, at that moment, we *can* go. It is a journey that, theoretically, like one's efforts to find an ultimate reality, never ends. Which may be why the final sketch in the book is entitled "Don't Try to Find Me." By doing so, we would only discover where the director once was, before he disappeared, dissolving like the photographer in *Blow-Up*, or, like Locke on the moviola screen, vanishing "off the frame."

·   ·   ·

Several cautions. First, these "sketches" are clearly not meant to be read as disjointed jottings or notes, random *aperçus* in search of a context or script in which to insert themselves. Nor are they imagistic mock-ups, preliminary outlines waiting to be developed. They are an extremely revealing and highly selective group—a progressive gallery, I would say—of narrative nuclei. Regarded as visual "stills," they are in some real sense satisfactory; but they all look forward to dynamic enlargement, a more ample fulfillment. Whether they take the form of storylike narratives (like "Toward the Frontier" and "The Desert of Money"), image-situations, or prose poems (like "In the Cup of a Lily"), they have all been *composed*; they exhibit that painstaking quest for accuracy and clarity so conspicuous in the director's films.

The collection as a whole has also been composed as a montage of Antonioni's most persistent themes. The order of the pieces is not chronologically structured, but rather designed to reveal the process by which a film grows from its matrix. The craftsmanlike finish of the prose tells us that, relatively speaking, these pieces have been completed. To an interviewer who asked what his intention was in writing them, Antonioni tersely replied, "To write them as well as possible." Not for the sake of literary virtuosity (to which he modestly makes no claim), but in the interests of the film to which they may (or may not) eventually lead and in which, as visual poetry, they aspire to fulfill themselves. Essentiality, purity of suggestion, the intimation of a mystery that lies beyond words, a clarity enabled by relentlessly stripping away any sensuous addition that might distract from the latent reality of the emerging image—this is their aim. They are not "roughs" precisely because the crucial larval stages in the making of a film have been completed in the writer's struggle to endow them with just this finish of composition.

Not all of them are, or were, destined to find fulfillment in a film. The piece entitled "Four Men at Sea," for instance, developed into a screenplay called *The Crew*, a film which Antonioni had hoped to shoot in 1984 and which then had to be shelved, at least temporarily, for lack of funding. In the meantime the director is reportedly shooting a script for television based on the nucleus included here under the title of "Two Telegrams." One, perhaps more, of the pieces in the book were absorbed by the script of *Tecnically Sweet** (*Tecnicamente dolce*), arguably the most ambitious script Antonioni has ever attempted and which,

---

* The script was drafted in 1966 and has now been published with a fine introduction by Aldo Tassone and a preface by Antonioni (Milan, 1974). The title comes from a remark made by the physicist Oppenheimer: "It is my opinion that if one catches sight of something that appears to him to be technically sweet, he attaches himself to it and does it." On that script Antonioni commented revealingly: "In the summer of 1966 I thought I had overcome everything. In

had it been shot, would almost certainly have proven the richest
and most thematically comprehensive film of his oeuvre. That
script was partly assimilated (along with its themes and proposed
lead actors, Jack Nicholson and Maria Schneider) in *The Passenger* (1974) and will almost certainly never be shot. Other nuclei
have presumably been permanently discarded; others are still
awaiting that privileged moment when they might develop into
scripts or be attracted into the orbit of other, more complex
aggregates.

.   .   .

That this is not mere mystification of the creative process is
confirmed by the exhibition of Antonioni's "paintings" entitled
Le montagne incantate (The Enchanted Mountains), shown at
the Galleria d'Arte Moderna in Rome in late 1983.* "Painting"
is not the right word since the exhibition consisted of a series of
drastic technological transformations of paintings by means of
photographic enlargement. The originals, all miniature gouaches
or collages, range in size from matchbox proportions to four by
nine inches of horizontal rectangle, approximating the dimensions of the cinemascope screen. The subjects are uniformly landscapes, or rather mountainscapes, rolling chains or snowy peaks
profiled against a horizon of varicolored sky. The mountains,
enchanted both *with* and *by* the horizon stretching beyond them,

---

that *battle between the film and myself* [translator's emphasis] I regarded myself
as the winner. But I had failed to take account of that implacable, pitiless, and
cynical arbiter who holds in his hands the thread of every cinematic enterprise—
the producer. When Carlo Ponti told me, unexpectedly and inexplicably, that
he no longer intended to produce the film, that he had changed his mind, the
world that I had so laboriously constructed in my mind, fantastic and true, so
beautiful and mysterious, suddenly crumbled. The ruins are still here. Somewhere inside me."

* The catalogue (*Antonioni: Le montagne incantate*), edited by Ida Panicelli
with prefatory remarks by various hands, was published by Electa Editrice
(Milan, 1983). While giving a good idea of Antonioni's paintings, they have the
unavoidable disadvantage of reversing the crucial technological process, reduc-
ing what has been so purposely enlarged, in order to fit the scale of the catalogue
format.

convey the ideas of walled enclosure but also of transcendence beyond the peak, a *varco* or passage toward the receding horizon—of constraint and possible freedom. These are then enlarged hundreds of times their original size; the resultant prints resemble the final blow-ups in *Blow-Up*—the grainy outline of a pistol barrel glinting among the leaves; the outline of a human form apparently moldering into the humus on which it lies. The viewer sees images which have been technologically exploded, violently projected into a new dimension, a different orography. The precision of outline in the originals is blurred; the boundary between mountain and sky, foreground and the mountain, remains, but the masses seem to be merging, interpenetrating. Solid colors decompose into *pointilliste* designs or designlessness. The textures change, producing in the enlargement a grainy, almost molecular quality, pullulating with movement. Both original and enlargements reveal the hand of a superbly scrupulous colorist, recalling Japanese and Chinese Zen landscapes, mysterious and beautiful, the balk of earth and snowy peaks blending with the clouds in the distance.

But in the enlargements, unlike the originals, there is a quality that can only be felt as violence—a violence which Antonioni explicitly intended. We sense it as the visual revelation of the exploded energies latent but dormant in the "stills" of the original paintings, as though some inward force, rendered visible by magnification, had suddenly, aggressively, declared itself; as though, to make use of the Eliot line cited in this book by Antonioni, we had been subjected to the discomfort of looking out the same window and seeing a different landscape; as though what had seemed solid, bright, and familiar had been forced to narrate its own hidden violence and inward uncertainty. The enlargements convey the sense of *active* mystery, of volcanically restless power concealed beneath the familiar outward features of what we once took for real.

The effect is not unlike that sought by Renaissance painters in what was called a "perspective," that is, that double reality obtained when the artist subjects familiar objects and scenes to the distorted perspective of anamorphosis. If the viewer of Holbein's *The Ambassadors* stands in just the right position to the far right of the painting, he will see that what, from the usual facing position, seems to be a shawl lying on the floor is in fact a human skull—the hidden *memento mori* suddenly revealed as the destiny of the two ambassadors, both seized by the painter in the prime of life and at the peak of their powers. Head-on, face to face, they confront *us* as we confront them, neither aware of what cannot be seen except by a drastic shift of perspective. Until that shift occurs, the viewer, like the photographer at the beginning of *Blow-Up* and the discontentedly groping Locke of *The Passenger*, is ruled by encoded perceptions and the lineaments of the conventionally given world. In the Holbein painting the rightly positioned viewer comes to recognize himself, just as he also recognizes the nature of the reality enclosing him within the familiar world defined by the frame, and which *within* the frame, is troubled only by those objects—a tiny crucifix on the wall at the edge of the world's green curtain, that strange shawl-like object lying on the floor—over which the routinely seeing eye quickly passes, mesmerized by the confident vitality and presence of the two ambassadors.

So too, in these exploded gouaches of Antonioni, the viewer is confronted with the *narrated*, kinetically documented reality of the two worlds in which he lives. Peace and violence, beauty and terror, familiar and mysterious, transient and eternal, prose and poetry, immanence and transcendence—all the old opposites, dynamically visualized in the arc of unfolding reality, made possible by combining artist's hand and technological process, confront each other. Not, it seems to me, as opposites, but rather as complementaries in pointed dialogue with each other. The artist's aim here, like the director's in his films, is not to juxtapose appearance with reality to the detriment of what is called "appearance," but instead to capture that metaphysical moment in which they combine. In order for that to happen, familiar reality—the world of common appearance—must be compelled to bring its latencies—its violence, mystery, and uncertainty—to light.

Antonioni's text for this kind of vision is a passage from the Roman poet Lucretius (who also provides the epigraph to *That Bowling Alley on the Tiber*). In his famous Cannes interview after the screening of *L'avventura* in 1959, Antonioni commented:

> Lucretius, who was certainly one of the greatest poets who ever lived, once said, "Nothing appears as it should in a world where nothing is certain. The only certain thing is the existence of a secret violence that makes everything uncertain." What Lucretius said of his time is still a disturbing reality, for it seems to me that this uncertainty is very much of our time.

It is worth recalling that the final shot of *L'avventura* shows the two lovers standing below the snowy peak of Mount Etna. Their drained faces express a kind of resolution, the calm of a temporary emotional plateau—a calm confirmed, it seems, by the snow-capped eternity and mass of Etna. But that emotional peace, as we know if we have seriously watched the film, is actually extremely precarious, as much at the mercy of the lovers' capacity for violent shifts of feeling as the giant calm of Etna—an "enchanted mountain" if ever there was one—is menaced by its own latent volcanic unrest. So too, in the first nucleus, "The Event Horizon," the human world stands in a complementary or perhaps analogous relation to the cosmos itself. Each world—this and that—contains its own constantly receding horizon, its apparent incongruities of beauty and violence, calm and turbulence, as well as its final mystery, the horizon of horizons, the black hole into which, if we imagine mountainscapes infinitely enlarged, visible reality vanishes, just as the human world disappears into the mystery of death, from which no information ever escapes.

There is still another way of putting the point. For Antonioni, titles, like credit lines, are an integral thematic part of the work. When this book was already in proofs, he suggested (too late for the suggestion to be adopted) that the title be changed to *A Pack*

of Lies or *Nothing But Lies*. His purpose, I take it, was to shift
the emphasis from the theme of violence to the creative process
involved in the notion of an embryonic nucleus, to persuade the
thoughtful reader to ask: In what way are these narrative nuclei
to be regarded as lies? By "lies" does he mean merely fictions?
And if they are lies, then what is the truth to which they give
the lie? To ask the question is clearly to answer it. The undeveloped, unrealized nucleus bears the same relation to the completed film as partial truth—always dependent on parody or dis-
tortion of reality, however unintentional, and to that extent an
effective falsehood—bears to the revealed truth. Truth is the
disclosure of the merely potential, as the oak is the dynamic
truth of the acorn. "I've always wanted," says Antonioni in one
of these tales, "to make a mechanism not of facts, but of
moments that recount the hidden tensions of those facts,
as blossoms reveal the fact of a tree." What counts then
is what Aristotle would have called *energia* or *praxis*, that
disclosure-in-movement which is par excellence the power of
cinema.

In short, there is no commitment here either to some naive
correspondence theory of the truth or to its fashionable opposite,
that what we mistakenly call "truth," "reality," and "meaning"
are fictions or illusions generated by our inability to escape the
web of encoded language in which we are forever hopelessly
entangled. Of *Zabriskie Point*, for instance, Antonioni remarked
that his purpose was to achieve "the aura of a fable," and that,
"even if critics object, I do believe one thing: fables are true."
True, because the tale succeeds, however briefly, in locating the
"metaphysical moment" (Antonioni's phrase) when subject and
object, particular and universal, transient and timeless, intersect
and fuse. The completed film may be a fiction, but it is precisely
that more ample fiction which, whatever theorists may hold, is
the truth *for now*. Truth, in short, is provisional. Reality, like
truth, like that horizon receding beyond the mountains, constantly eludes our grasp and our optics. "When we think we've
achieved it [reality]," Antonioni remarked apropos of *Blow-Up*,

the situation is already different. By developing with enlargers an
image shot in a setting where light is scarce [i.e., by latensification],
you succeed in obtaining a shining image. As we go deeper with
this process, we probably arrive at the true reality of things. Things
emerge that we probably don't see with the naked eye. I always
distrust what I see because I imagine what lies beyond it. And that
there is an image beyond this which we don't know. The photographer in *Blow-Up*, who is not a philosopher, wants to see things
closer up. But it so happens that, by enlarging too far, the object
itself decomposes and disappears. Hence there's a moment in which
we grasp reality, but then the moment passes. This was in part the
meaning of *Blow-Up*. . . .

Reality, like truth, is attainable, but only temporarily, provisionally so. This provisional truth is true in part because it points
to its own transcendence in a larger truth, to the image that lies
beyond it. Or, speaking biologically or anthropologically (as Antonioni often does), we might say that it is *instrumentally* true,
that without it we cannot live or transcend ourselves, cannot
adapt to a changing world where "the only certain thing is uncertainty." It is necessary to life, the instrument by which, in
Nietzsche's Darwinian sense, man evolves, by which he *became*,
and must go on *becoming*, himself. He can't, without ceasing to
be human, kick the habit of meaning.

"I believe in improvisation," Antonioni persists in telling his
doubting critics. Which presupposes a faith in the provisional
nature of life and artistic truth as registered by the candid and
courageous improviser. Insofar as the director admits that reality
keeps eluding us, receding as soon as we catch sight of it, he is
committed to the inherent tragedy of his quest, but at the same
time he reveals in that art, which is himself, the virtues—patience, courage, amplitude of vision, self-sacrifice, compassion—
which are generated by that tragedy and which constitute its
unfolded truth.

Until then, art lies. Photographically, that unfolded lie might be
compared to the murk in which we mostly live our lives. We, like

these undeveloped nuclei, are mere latencies. We begin to emerge from this dark, undifferentiated world, to find individuated form, by a process of latensification, as when a latent image is revealed by a chemical process or subjected to low intensities of light. Humanly and artistically, this process requires struggle, suffering, even violence. Change and growth are, like birth, painful. Love, like thinking, often hurts. The contents of the unconscious are not brought to light without struggle. In all metamorphosis and transcendence, whether biological, historical, personal, or artistic, there is a component of violence. The cinema that takes truth as both its aspiration and its generic justification will be a cinema born of that metaphysical violence that triggers the explosive charge latent in such nuclei as these and propels them toward their fulfillment in the director and in us.

The director's greatest danger, according to Antonioni, is cinema's extraordinary capacity for telling lies. Its synesthetic power is so great that its capacity for falsifying the world is almost unlimited—above all in a mass society, with its industrialized entertainments, the semiotic bombardment of commercial capitalism and consumerism, competing ideologies with organized systems of "disinformation," and the increasing aversion of mass audiences to arduous complexities of feeling and thought. But the greater danger is that cinema may, by lending its powers to mass-produced falsehoods, manufactured clichés, political simplifications, hi-tech optimism, and the distortions of ideologies, forfeit its own immense capacities for registering, perhaps even revealing, the truth. Film may sell its soul. Its potentialities are extraordinary—those of the most comprehensive and complex medium ever invented by the human mind. Yet, as a consequence of its own misuse of those powers, by its prostitution to the entertainment industry and its haplessly conditioned audience, it is increasingly perceived as an immense mechanism for profitable lying, for evading all contact with reality, for, in short, maximizing and disseminating what the Italians call *robaccia*: junque.

.   .   .

By tentatively visualizing how one of these nuclei might be developed, the curious reader will obtain an imaginative sense of their intrinsic visual values and thematic density as well as their potential for cinematic poetry.

Consider, for instance, "Toward the Frontier." The starting point, as so often in Antonioni, is a situation of enclosure, of cramping confinement. The director with three colleagues has been locked in a hotel room in Merano to complete a Visconti script. Somehow freed of his task, he decides to go on an evening's *scampagnata* with three casual friends—an Italian girl, a German woman, and an American officer. Crowded into a jeep—confinement again—they head for the Austrian frontier. The time, we might suppose, is early evening; the bulk of the Alps is still profiled against the darkening sky. The horizon beckons; they feel the exhilaration of release, the anticipation of an evening's freedom and pleasure. But they are also separated by differences of culture and language, frontiers which must be crossed with tact if not caution. Forced intimacy (as in the yacht sequence at the beginning of *L'avventura*) gradually produces undercurrents of half-formed feelings, incipient emotions, tentative gestures, and brings them to the surface. As the darkness gathers outside and in the jeep, the headlights go on. Reassuringly. They arrive at a Tyrolean *Gasthaus*, and the strangeness of the place and its inhabitants increase their sense of discomfort and awkwardness, driving them closer together. The narrating camera presumably explores *them* as they explore the *Gasthaus* and each other. Slowly they begin to recognize their actual situation: intruders in an alien world, erotic and emotional smugglers in a world of real smugglers, aliens among aliens (again the closeness to *L'avventura*, the island sequence, with its smugglers and erotic undercurrents). But they have *chosen* to come on this trip, toward this horizon, this unwelcoming *Gasthaus*. Destination, as so often in Antonioni, is destiny. People insert themselves into geographies or situations that express their own internal reality.

So their own earlier exhilaration of release gives way to a renewed feeling of enclosure, but this time in an alien space—

a situation where the intruders begin to feel and act like participants, not merely observers, incipient accomplices in the drama
of mystery and violence beginning to gather around them. They
are entangled like willingly conscript actors, in an unraveling
plot whose outcome, unknown to them, lies within them. The
recognition scene takes place in a valley clearing in the forest,
in the sepulchral light cast by the moon now rising over the
peaks, revealing the horizon. In this setting, in this strange half-
light, they hear, and partly witness, a crime of murderous passion
which is, at least potentially given the gathering momentum of
their feelings, their own. (The situation, as the director notes,
is remarkably close to that of *Blow-Up*.) But it is this darker
world with its uncanny light (the director's own world once, as
his intruded wartime experience in an Abruzzi village makes
clear) that the driver-director now consciously and purposely
enters. The decision is registered in typically Antonioni fashion,
not verbally but visually. Making a decisive U-turn, away from
Merano and toward the border, cutting off the ignition and those
headlights that have hitherto illuminated his way, he plunges
downhill toward the densely forested frontier, along the moonlit
road, toward that darker Austria, that *selva oscura* whose horizon
is now his destination and, one assumes, that of his passengers
too.

All very conjectural, to be sure. And admittedly, in Antonioni's
words, "Any explanation would be less interesting than the mystery itself." But hypothetical as it may be, even this bare-bones
scenario may serve to suggest the essential features of the director's film-making. The heart of the nucleus is unmistakably
the epiphany of strange violence in the valley. We don't know—
we participants, we readers—precisely what happens, merely
that where two figures stood at odd angles to each other in the
moonlit clearing, one now lies on the ground. There is no causal
link whatever between this event and the lives of the intruders
from Merano who witness it. Nothing whatsoever, at least in
ordinary cinematic terms, happens in this scenario, nothing except this dimly perceived event. In another, essentially poetic,

sense, *everything* has happened. One life, perhaps three lives, perhaps more (the lives of the smugglers whose activities were suddenly interrupted by the intruders' arrival in the *Gasthaus*, and that of the murdered woman) have been changed forever. Above all that of the director-driver, whose coordinate but different lives—like those of Dante the poet and Dante the pilgrim—overlap and inform each other's. The director *qua* director enters an unknown "landscape," a mysterious world that we can reasonably suppose disturbs his technical complacencies, his confidence in the conventional modes of preparing a script and writing a story, even of shooting it. He sets out, he doesn't quite know why, for "the frontier," that mysterious world we see with his eyes and ours, opening up around him, a world that reveals, not the prefabricated mystery of a traditional "mystery story," but the much darker mystery latent in ordinary lives and unscrutinized events. As driver-participant, he enters a world where he must acknowledge the existence of feelings—of suppressed and to that degree illicit passion, even a potential inward violence—suddenly revealed to him as he too crosses the frontier of his unexplored relations to others, his awkward discomfort of finding himself at odd angles to *them*. Something in him, as in the director, some antecedent discomfort with the stale reality in which he has been confined, leads him to this outing and then, as his deeper feelings begin to "latensify," he makes his conscious decision to continue the journey, even though this may mean immersing himself in "the destructive element."

Small vivid details would presumably support the new complication of his feelings toward the others. Details like those patterned majolica tiles whose arabesques reach out to the borders of the adjoining tiles, where the pattern is broken, incapable of merging with the counterpart pattern in the surrounding tiles. The whole procedure is intrinsically that of visual poetry: poetry because it works by analogies and the perception of noncausal links hidden beneath the apparently placid surface of ordinary events—links all the more potent for being concealed, for their real *suppression* and therefore their explosive power when suddenly liberated. Here, in this suppression, lies the violence that makes its epiphany in the eerie light of the clearing, numinous with a meaning that cannot be decoded except in the gathering undercurrents of feeling that have now precipitated it. The forest, the mountainscape, the Faustian equipment—car and head-lights—that have hitherto been their means of penetrating the darkness which is now their world and destination, declare their meaning in the narrative equivalent of Bill's abstraction in *Blow-Up*—a metaphysical landscape where things have not yet begun to sort themselves out, a dark field illuminated by a few scattered points of light. Their own interior world has been projected into the phenomenal world where they can, like us, presumably for the first time, see it objectified, or at least limned.

"Inside of us," Antonioni has said, "things appear like dots of light in backgrounds of fog and shadow. Our concrete reality has a ghostly abstract quality." *This* is chaotic abstraction out of which Antonioni's metaphysical itineraries all begin. Whether as a fantasy of escape, a walk through the city, a journey across a desert, a plane in a cloud-bank or shattered by storms, a boat passing, a rocket, even a spaceship—all these real or longed-for voyages express the distance to be traversed, by those characters willing or discontented enough to make the journey, between the world in which they find themselves trapped and that horizon that beckons them toward freedom, that engages the would-be trav-eler's energies and his yearning to transcend both his condition and himself. The journey begins, as we saw, with an abstraction of an actual condition—a sense of acute disorder represented as a background of fog and shadow in which "things appear like dots of light." The abstraction slowly sorts itself out and an emerg-ing pattern is detected. Forms individuate themselves, take on distinctness and chroma. Certainties gradually establish them-selves, then harden into conventions, codified reality. The cod-ified order thus achieved later begins to weigh us down again, to suppress another abstraction stirring in our depths, the prob-lematics, gathering explosively beneath our surface certainties, which we can then project and objectify as a new horizon. Like the outworn or discarded pattern, it too is lit by a ghostly light; all one can see at this stage are those *pointilliste* dottings with perhaps the merest faint suggestion of a figurative latency, a new pattern, emerging.

The "return" to the horizon of abstraction is of course not really a return at all, but an advance into a new murk, a new dimension that eludes our perception and understanding even as we advance. We move, like the photographer in *Blow-Up*, like Locke in *The Passenger* (and of course like Antonioni, from film to film), from where we *were*, stripping ourselves of the baggage that encumbers our journey, to where we *are*, into this new abstraction with its eerie light, its dangerous Lucretian uncertainty and secret violence, born of the new uncertainties which our old certainties suppressed. This is, I believe, the master pattern, the kinetic life of Antonioni's design. In the words of T. S. Eliot, with whose vision of a similar (though more religious) pattern Antonioni feels such affinity:

> *We shall not cease from exploration*
> *And the end of all our exploring*
> *Will be to arrive where we started*
> *And know the place for the first time*

Atlanta, Georgia   William Arrowsmith
August 1985

THAT BOWLING ALLEY
ON THE TIBER

Quod si iam rerum ignorem primordia quae sint,
hoc tamen ex ipsis caeli rationibus ausim
confirmare aliisque ex rebus reddere multis
nequaquam nobis divinitus esse paratam
naturam rerum: tanta stat praedita culpa.[1]

LUCRETIUS, *De rerum natura*, V, 195–99

The event horizon

ONE November morning a few years back I was flying over Soviet Central Asia. I was looking out over the endless desert bounding the Aral sea to the east, white and sluggish, and thinking of the film (*The Kite*) I'd be shooting in these parts next spring. A story, a world that's never been mine, that's why I like it. And while thinking of this story, watching it obediently attach itself to the landscape, I felt my thoughts sliding far away. It's always the same. Every time I start working on one film, another one comes to mind.

This new film originated in a trip in a small plane, in Italy, a day of bad weather. Enormous clouds, rain, wind. A stubborn, persistent wind, gray as the clouds. Outside the window the clouds go whizzing past. The plane's tossing brutally, bucking, unpredictably swerving. With a little patience, one gets used even to danger. Quite suddenly, the clouds stop, we have the feeling that the plane is falling. Instead, it's being tossed upward where just now there was a flash of lightning. Earlier the intensity of the gray was caused by the dense cloud-pack, now by the flashes of yellow lightning that tear it apart.

We pass through five storms. On our arrival I'm informed that another tourist plane had crashed in the fourth storm. No survivors. It was carrying six passengers and the pilot.

An industrialist, chemical sector, and his wife. He'd taken his degree in chemistry but remembered very little. He'd married for love. He used to explain that he'd made a mistake for love. Just suppose, he used to say to his wife, if someday we had children who were as much strangers to us as we are to each other. Before he left, they had an argument. The husband went off, slamming the door. In the room the silence fell. And in that silence she noticed with horror that during the whole argument she'd remained in the same posture as he.

A writer. He'd taken a course in rapid reading. Two hundred lines a minute. But when he was writing he was very slow. He never tired of correcting the page and then reading it over. He used to read over his published books, each time with renewed hope, and then with prompt disappointment, shelve them again. He worshipped reality, but when he wrote, all connection between reality and literary imagination vanished. He began to make less and less use of the latter. Besides, reading had been the grand passion of his youth. At the time of the energy crisis, he used to read at night in front of the window by the light of a streetlamp. At midnight only the alternate lights were lit. His was one of those that were put out. He was already famous when he met the industrialist and his wife. He immediately sent her one of his novels. He'd not seen her again subsequently, not the least word nor even a telephone call. He was surprised and flattered by the invitation to go on the trip; it might have been she who instigated it. But at the airport a glance told him how wrong he was, and that the subject of his novel wouldn't even be mentioned. To reduce his humiliation, he chose the course of nonchalance. It lasted very briefly. Going up the hatchway, he noticed another writer's novel in the wife's bag. And this struck him as so tactless that he chose a seat in the rear, far away from her. Besides, he thought, I'm safer in the rear.

The writer's mistress. Obsessed by her figure and by death. She'd written to a famous French biologist to ask him straight out to define death. Death is a statistical hypothesis, the biologist had replied, sincerely yours, etc. I don't think that this answer settles the issue, the writer commented. He was totally uninterested in the problem. His advice was that it's better not to

think about it. She looked at him with contempt, slipping the
pocket notebook back into her handbag. It's too easy to talk about
death only to say that it's better not to think about it, she said.
This took place while they were setting out for the airport. On
the first page of her notebook was written: Please send to, and
her name and address. She'd foreseen that it would be lost. It
was found, however, in the middle of a clump of red clover, with
that useless address quite visible, written in caps.

A former Member of Parliament in his forties. Summoned as
a defense witness in a civil suit, he'd gone to the court a few
hours before the departure, suitcase in hand. The trial dealt with
a young man who'd murdered his nineteen-year-old wife out of
jealousy. The young man declared that the girl had confessed to
having a lover, and that his lover was the M.P. He denied it.
The accused was sentenced to twenty-six years in prison. His
age at the time was twenty-five, so he'd be fifty-two when he
was let out. When the former M.P. heard the sentence, he was
overwhelmed by a sharp sense of pain and responsibility. But
when he thought of the murdered girl, he felt tender and transferred the pain to her. He was a gentle man. He had an extremely
good memory of the women who had rejected him.

A lady of a certain age, attractive, unmarried. She'd just returned from the Rostov Fair in Russia, where she'd bought a
two-year old Budennyi stallion. She'd paid $180,000. On the day
before her trip with her friends a painful case of hypertension
had led her to consult a doctor. The doctor prescribed a laxative.
A laxative? You won't believe it, he'd explained, but even an
ordinary cathartic can produce in us a state of tranquil lassitude,
thereby deflecting our normal aggressiveness and inducing meditation. Even before the laxative took effect, the explanation gave
her a curious sense of tranquillity. But when she spoke of the
incident on the phone with the former M.P., a phrase of his
warned her that her tension was still very near the surface. Have
faith in science, the man suggested, it's better for me that you
not be aggressive tomorrow, I have a proposition to make you.
What proposition, she would have liked to ask him right then,

alarmed. But she said nothing. She dropped her arm without hanging up and stayed there listening to the voice at the other end of the line saying hello, hello, hello . . .

The pilot. A complicated soul, indecisive, full of apprehensions. He woke up in the morning unhappy with himself. When the maid brought him the newspapers, he read them in an instant, angrily. And then telephoned someone to argue about what he'd read. If the other person disagreed with him, he insulted him. But if he agreed, there was a silence. The day of the trip he was strangely serene. He had talked with a woman on the phone. After the call, he left for the airport. To be noted: his cheerful Good Morning to a woman in mourning.

The plane crashed five thousand feet above sea level. The sea can be glimpsed in the distance through a gap of dark rock, but only rarely do the shepherds stop along the path to look at it. If they stop, it's at sunset, since the sunset in some way recapitulates the weary labors of their day. The shepherds live a stone's throw from the spot where the plane crashed. There are two or three hundred of them, nobody's ever counted them. Plus two carabinieri and a priest.

When the priest arrives on the spot, a strong wind is still blowing. The corporal's already there but doesn't know what to do. The priest doesn't know either. In the doctor's absence it's his task to take care of the sick and wounded of the high plateau. But there's nothing here except unrecognizable remains scattered in the grass, so let's concern ourselves with souls, thinks the priest. And he starts praying. From the village others come also, to look. Death is a spectacle that costs nothing, that attracts. This time it offers little—a burnt fuselage, shreds of human beings, on the meadow traces of a probable attempt to land. The shepherds watch, they're used to silence, a few words and they leave. The priest disappears too. The corporal's left alone.

He's a young man who comes from the north, like that day's storms. He'd gladly leave too, if it weren't for a vague sense of duty and that clean wind, which he knows well and which makes his work less painful. The event has made a deep and confusing impression on him. Confusing because he lacks the particulars. How many dead? Who are they? Above all, where are they? Near the fuselage there's almost nothing, it's obvious that the plane must have exploded on impact and everything inside was hurled violently about. Even farther off, within a radius of sixty yards, there's little more. Maybe the pilot was the only person on board. The hypothesis immediately collapses. In the midst of his searching, the sergeant suddenly spots something colored, some torn shreds of a woman's dress. And nearby, in a clump of red clover, a small notebook. He picks it up, reads the letters written in caps. He leafs through it. On today's date, underlined several times, are these words: What time? They're written sideways across the page by a nervous hand, leading one to suspect an astonishing presentiment. But that's not the sort of suspicion the corporal can entertain. The fact that one of the dead now has a name, and that this is a woman's name, strikes him more strongly. And in his mind he projects a series of women's faces which by turns juxtapose themselves with that name. The corporal chooses one of them, borrowed perhaps from a magazine, and his projection stops there.

He also stops searching. The dead, the shreds and pulp of the dead, are irrecoverable. Except for two fingers at the end of the meadow toward the sea. The fingers are attached to a piece of a hand, an oddly neat man's hand, and they grip a little white plastic coffee spoon. They're slightly curved and they're holding the spoon turned downward in the usual gesture of mixing. Below, in place of the cup, there's a bloodstain, as though in such a situation it made more sense to mix blood than coffee. It's this logic, the very banality of it, that makes the composition terrifying. The corporal detaches his gaze and looks toward the woods.

The high plateau is surrounded by woods, very green in all seasons. The green is barely diminished by the chestnut tint of the trunks and the black of the shadows, so it's completely dominant, except for the opening toward the sea with its changing color. The green is tender or bold or gloomy, as now. This then is the scenario: thunderheads in the sky, on the ground a shattered plane and the dead. It's a serious corner of the world. A tiny piece of nameless earth where the infinite game which man is forbidden to understand is re-enacted.

There are two men now. The second has unexpectedly appeared a little way off, where the woods begin. They're of different age, background, education. One wears a carabiniere's uniform, the other a business suit. In the field of the frame, from a slight high angle perhaps, the first man is on the left with his back almost to the viewer, the second on the right, is facing us. They're both motionless, absorbed. They look at the same sad, silent things in front of them and no doubt they both think, each in his own way, the same thought: How in the world did events happen for these people in this way? All men who look at death are the same man. But it's an identity that lasts only for that look, the first gesture annuls it. As soon as he realizes that he's no longer alone, the corporal approaches the newcomer and asks: Are you a relative? No, the other replies. His tone of voice is so firm that the corporal doesn't know what to answer. It's that way with the answers given by his superiors, they leave nothing to ask. Anyway, what else can he ask? What's left for him to do? He's notified his superiors, it's up to them to make the decisions. The only order they've given him is to prevent relatives—in case they get to the scene first—from touching or moving the remains, so as not to hinder the inquest. But the man seems to have no such intention. He wanders back and forth, looking. Looking's not forbidden.

A piece of a high-quality handbag at the edge of the wood tells him that they were rich folk: fine-scaled alligator leather, a boar-skin lining, buckle of matte metal, and the man's two fingers, the way they hold the spoon, the manicured nails. By now he has a good eye for details. Once a street-cleaner explained to him how to distinguish the garbage of poor neighborhoods from that of the residential quarters. Silver paper on boxes of chocolate, pineapple parings, wilted gardenias, labels from bottles of San Gemini water and French cognac, cabbage leaves . . . Nothing of all this in the garbage of the poor. The poor eat the cabbage leaves.

Tomorrow, with the arrival of inquiring relatives, curiosity-seekers, journalists, he would find out who these rich people were. But this isn't the moment yet for giving the facts the importance they deserve. I insist on saying that these are notes and that what interests me at this stage is to clarify the story I'm telling. That might appear an epistemological way of attacking the plot, but matter has become a shadow not only in physics (because of relativity and the uncertainty principle), but also in everyday reality. It's not for nothing that mathematicians, used to calling things by their right names, designate the unknown with the symbol X. If I try to define the X of the film I'm speaking of, I'm led to concentrate on a reflection made by the man who last entered the action. It so happens that he makes this reflection when, tired of busying himself with the dead, he finds himself thinking about the living, about himself, about all the people who've invaded the plateau.

Because of his work, this man has recently had contact with physicists, astronomers, astrophysicists, cosmologists. He's heard them talk of galactic tides, absolute magnitude, solar storms, pulsars, quasars, cosmic rays, interstellar molecules, and of course black holes. Invisible objects that bend space and warp time, fragments of primordial matter enclosed in a sphere of energy from which nothing escapes unless it reaches, and surpasses, the unreachable speed of light. Now, what has struck him most is the definition of this sphere, this implacable horizon. It's called the "event horizon."[2]

What disturbs him is the fact that the same term is used to indicate events of cosmic importance, which can't even be observed even though they obey systems of basic physical hypotheses, and others like the convergence of events that brought these persons, dead and living, to this place. The shepherds who've come back to see the spectacle of sorrow. The carabinieri from the city with a sergeant to give an appearance of order to contingency. Journalists, no more than two, dispatched here to see if any of the victims is worth writing about. He's also disturbed by the fact that the word "horizon" is applied not only to the woods, the mountains and sea that surround the plateau, but also to that line separating our world from the gravitational field of the black hole, which thereby remains cut off from the world. And also that it might not be black at all, but a ball of fire no bigger than an atom. He's read stupefying things on this topic. And it's not without irony that he now recalls them, in relation to what happens around him. The passengers on the crashed plane are also enclosed in the landscape which fuses with the horizon of their little events, and they too have slipped down toward a state of death. It's been said that the story of astronomy is a story of receding horizons. But for human life the horizon has remained fixed.

Engrossed in these thoughts, the man hasn't noticed the approach of the journalists. Nobody knows who he is or what he's doing there, and they have questions to ask him. Ask away, says the man. Once again irony comes to his aid. It seems to him that, at this moment, it's the only way of saving himself. The light too comes to his aid. The clouds have thickened and cast a livid shadow on the spectacle unfolding on the plateau. An ordinary setting, the man thinks. He goes on replying to the questions in a half-serious tone and meanwhile lets his eyes pan around and then up, to look at the clouds. Beyond the clouds.

At twenty or twenty-five thousand feet the sky is always blue. Then the blue stops and the darker blue begins, growing ever more intense. One hundred and thirty miles up the sky is black. Stars, galaxies, nebulas, clusters, radio-galaxies billions of light-years distant, gas and dust fill it almost completely. And all of it receding from us at insane speed. But not only from us, because the recession is isotropic. If this recession goes on indefinitely, that means that the universe is open, infinite. If it someday stops or changes direction, then it's closed, finite. In short, even the universe has its event horizon. With this peculiarity, that it's the ultimate horizon, the horizon of horizons beyond which there are no other events, no longer anything.

It's also been said: But if man had to go beyond what he can understand, what would be the purpose of the sky?

Antarctic

THE Antarctic glaciers are moving in our direction at a rate of three millimeters per year. Calculate when they'll reach us. Anticipate, in a film, what will happen.

Two telegrams

SHE was born and grew up wealthy, in the country. Her countryside is moist, fertile, like that of northern Italy, but more rugged. Her childhood was full of prohibitions, from which she emerged a taciturn girl, devoid of irony and girlfriends. Sensitive in her own way. Overwhelmed at times by bursts of enthusiasm for herself and her possibilities. Now she's a woman subject to being happy or unhappy, almost always for the same reasons. A woman more in need of conflict than harmony. The indifference of Nature was the dramatic discovery of her adolescence. It wasn't enough for her to look at those vast green and yellow landscapes, she wanted somehow to be part of them, to upset their undulations, their cadences. The various movements of the winds in the sky were for her a cause of frustration. Today, at forty, she feels herself betrayed when she thinks that there even ought to be somebody who succeeds in living his life.

She doesn't like people, especially if they show too much warmth of feeling. She detests people who gush. The thing that most pleases her in her husband is the size of his forehead because it gives her the feeling of toughness. She has a tender personal idea of ugliness as regards people and things. She'd like her relations to others to be less bound to conventions. She'd like other people always to be a little drunk. But her husband is abstemious, abstemious in general. Euphoria is unknown to him. Even his sexual extroversion is gloomy. This is why she betrays him. The first time with a man whom she leaves as soon as she sees she doesn't love him, and the second time with a man she leaves for the opposite reason. She's a woman who's ashamed of her own emotions. She hides them, disguises them, and in this way contradicts them. She's not even sure she feels them, these emotions. Maybe they're no use to her. She tries substituting different feelings, like going to parties where the guests, completely naked, indulge in promiscuous relations, or even sexually initiating the thirteen-year-old son of a woman friend of hers.

This episode changes the boy's life and her own. The boy's father is pleased that his son is sexually initiated. Less pleased by it having been done by a woman of her age. To get rid of her, he severs his friendship with her. In the effort to rekindle the friendship, she makes the worst mistake of all; she offers herself to him, almost without knowing what she's doing. But the father knows very well, he acquires a taste for it. But at this point it's she who pulls back and, to confirm her attitude, confesses everything to his wife, thus losing her friendship.

From that moment on, she shuts herself in a circle of respectability from which infidelities, lies, and eccentricities are excluded. She looks for and finds a job suited to her degree in chemistry and performs it scrupulously. Her office is in a skyscraper. Prefab walls, aluminum, plate glass, neon. A perfect grayness.

The first time I saw her she was simply a woman who'd stopped at a gas station. Gas stations have a large number of shiny surfaces. Whenever the woman found herself reflected in them, she was startled. She looked around as though she were frightened or hurrying. She orders five gallons, then three. She refuses to have her windshield cleaned. She opens her purse, shuts it, opens it again. She pays, her movements are jerky. Her dress was in hopeless bad taste.

The gas station is two minutes from her office. The woman parks in the space reserved for the building and, after a lightning trip up in the elevator, sits down at her desk. From the big window one sees, as on a wide screen, an angular urban view, hard, the color of skyscrapers. Thousands of windows that never open but revive one by one when the sun hits the street. The woman waits a bit before calling the secretary or reading the afternoon's correspondence or telephoning. When she begins, these habitual actions and the familiar surroundings help her recover her self-control. Her colleagues and staff also affectionately guide her toward it. In fact, they manage to make her smile. Little by little an icy calm takes possession of her.

Before she went down to the gas station, there was a knock at her door. It was her secretary with a telegram. The woman opens the telegram with a pair of scissors which she then puts on the desk, by chance in a spot the sun is just touching. She doesn't read the telegram. She sits there watching the sunlight crawl toward the scissors. The telephone rings. By the time the woman decides to answer it, the sun has already gone past the scissors and is approaching the edge of the desk. The call is from her husband, who asks her if she's gotten his telegram. Ah, it's from you? She's annoyed by the thought of the expected affectionate phrases of the message. She has no reason to think that this is what they are, but this is the idea that comes to her, the presentiment of a new conflict with reality. In fact, her husband has something else to ask her, something poorly suited to the metallic tone of the receiver: divorce.

The woman says nothing. She literally finds nothing to say. The words have a meaning when there's a face in front of you to which you can reply, or evade the words, or not speak. But instinctively she's turned her head away, her mouth is no longer close to the speaker. The connection with her husband is cut. All he hears is an immense astonishment.

She hangs up the receiver and lets her eyes fall on the telegram. The phrases she's just heard are repeated there, with a final ironic addition: I kiss you now, it's the only thing we can honestly and decently do.

It's at this point that the woman goes down to the gas station.

Inside the office it's already night. In a little while it will be dark outside. The colors quickly drain away. The difference in the light outside prevents the glass from reflecting the inside and the view imposes itself: static, indifferent. It doesn't even give back her own image.

The woman would gladly go out if only she could find a good reason for doing so. But her husband is waiting for her at home, he'll obviously be worried about the scene that will follow their meeting. Alright, so he's at home. So he's waiting for her. He's the last person she wants to see.

The employees have gone. They came to say goodnight and they've gone. In the ensuing silence she shuts her eyes and listens to the sound of the traffic and the wind that's now gusting. Up high, where she is, it's always windy. It's the wind that carries up this roaring of cars and this other prolonged whistling. It's the wind again, making the skyscraper sway and making her slightly dizzy.

The woman moves a few steps. She notices that the direction she's taken leads to a small table by the window and she moves more quickly, goes to light a lamp under a lightshade. A cone of violent light falls on the black of the table. Now the grouping—table, armchair, shade, woman—is distinctly mirrored in the window. The rest of the office is in shadow. The woman rises and disappears into this shadow, toward the desk. From the desk she starts turning on the overhead lights. They're directional lights that focus on circumscribed areas. By lighting them, each space is projected in the window and beyond the window, outside. It's as though the woman were throwing the office out the window, piece by piece. Herself included.

Maybe she'd actually like hovering in the air in order to reach, as in Andersen's fairy tale, the shadow of a man who keeps moving back and forth in the rectangle of a window in the skyscraper opposite. It's a very tall, dark building. But at night a white light bathes it, veiling the ghostly emptiness. That restless figure gives the woman an uneasiness she can't explain. She knows the name of the firm that occupies the whole floor, she doesn't know who the man is, she's never been in that office. But whoever he is, his presence seems to her to have an enormous value, what she doesn't know. The important thing now is to keep him from leaving, as he may be intending to do. To keep him there at all costs. She looks for the firm's number in the directory and dials it. She waits thirteen rings. And then lets the receiver drop, as though it were a weight. Her hand is tired. While resting it on the arm of the chair, her gaze falls on her husband's telegram. She immediately picks up the receiver and dials another number, three numbers. After a moment, knitting her brows and slightly raising her voice as she does with her secretary, she dictates a telegram. The address is that of the building opposite her, the message a phrase which includes the word "immediately" and a telephone number, her own.

An hour later the telegram is delivered. She realizes it when she sees the man standing at the window looking out. It's obvious that he's trying to identify her. With all the lights behind her lit, her silhouette must stand out sharply. In fact the man does see her. But instead of rushing to the telephone as she expected, he raises the window halfway and lets the telegram drop into the void.

Oddly the paper glides into the middle and starts falling, fluttering in the bottomless gorge. A stronger gust makes it spin but only for an instant, the telegram somehow frees itself from the vortex and takes refuge in a nook between one building and another, is then sucked up and then down again, is struck by the neon light, and glides away in sync with an indistinct sound. All the laws of physics at work there outside seem to be ganging up against it. The woman follows it until it disappears, but even afterward she goes on listening. She wants to hear the imperceptible thud of the telegram touching ground and the garbage truck immediately carrying it away. Along with all her hopes.

The man's disappeared. The woman goes back to her desk. A little later, when sleep comes and she dozes off with her head leaning on an elbow and a light directly over her head, she seems to be sleeping on the abyss beyond the window, in an office smashed to pieces. While she's asleep, it starts raining.

It rains till dawn. Instead of cleaning the air, the thunderstorm dirties it, leaving a veil of dust on the glass. Through this veil the view seems out of focus, unreal; tap with a finger on the window, and the view moves. Borges would say this woman is suffering from unreality. She can't even manage to definewhat she feels. The void of a few hours earlier is filled with a vague but persistent consciousness, with a thought of that long provocation her life has been. Of the indifference of Nature, from which she's suffered since childhood, to the indifference of things, of even the commonest objects like the pen with which she writes, the scissors, her house keys, her house. Does anything exclude a person more than houses where other people live, those possessors of absolute indifference?

A few of them will arrive at the office shortly. Her secretary, the employees, the security guards. As strangers. The day before they induced her to be calm in order to be calm *themselves*. This inference seems to her so strikingly clear that all her rancor and hatred for her husband vanish and in their place there slowly rises, like smoke in muggy air, a new feeling, a new kind of hatred, a sort of mass hatred that she relishes more.

I didn't make this film[3] because at a certain moment the character of the woman, which was something I knew intimately, seemed unpleasant to me and ultimately unacceptable. It happened that every time I reread the story, the inferences I drew from it were of a different sort, political even. Or rather, on the narrative and visual level, I liked it, but not conceptually.

But if I had made it, it would have been the film of this night, of this intersection of lonelinesses. Of this relation between inside and outside. With a culmination in which we see the woman mechanically grasp the scissors and go and stand beside the door. The office produces the first sounds of the morning, steps, voices. Some of these steps approach, stop outside the door. Someone has brought them this far. More than one. She hears them whispering, breathing. In a few seconds they'll enter.

Gripping the scissors in both hands, the woman raises her arms, ready to strike. No matter who. One of them.

The silence

AT the beginning a dialogue, a brief one, which will clarify a breakdown in relations concealed for years by both husband and wife. The usual habits, the usual hurt. But now that—by chance—they've at least begun to open up, the woman wants to have it all out.

"It's over, admit it. That way everything will be out in the open and we'll know what to do. It's enough to know what we want. Isn't that so? Answer me. Isn't that right?"

The husband nods without saying a word. She's silent too. Now that everything's out in the open, now that they're being honest, they have nothing more to say to each other.

A story of husband and wife who have nothing more to say to each other. Just once to shoot not their conversation but their silences, their silent words. Silence as a negative dimension of speech.

This body of filth

AMONG the books I've lent and not recovered there's one I'd like to get back more than all the others. It had a white jacket and the title was black. It looked like a headstone. Because of that title too, which sounded like an epitaph: *My Delight*. It was the diary of a cloistered nun. The nun was American. Of the Carmelite order. I have no interest in ascetism. I'm interested in irrationality. I believe that reason alone is incapable of explaining reality. As it can't explain cloistered seclusion.

I'd managed to convince an influential priest to get me admitted, disguised as a stonemason, into a cloistered convent. Spending a few days within those walls, breathing the same air that kept life in those women who had renounced life, seemed to me the first step. The priest was agreeable and even found the right place, a small monastery in a north Italian city. But he didn't agree with the idea that nuns were women who had renounced life. He was a cultivated man and the terms of the dilemma didn't escape him. On one hand, everything that gives a meaning to our existence, on the other the denial that all this has a meaning. Moreover, a profound contempt for our values, our objects, our feelings.

Cloistered monasteries, they say (that priest and others) are communities of prayer, sacrifice, and love. If we are to find in this trinomial answer to the practical reality of their existence, we need to know the meaning of prayer, sacrifice, and love. The cloistered nuns gather together the beseechings of the world and translate them into a colloquy with God. A thousand reasons seem to demonstrate the essential uselessness of a life spent in voluntary seclusion, the illusory nature of a devoted commitment to the world's salvation but that shuns the world in the most absolute way. Still, on the religious plane a thing's usefulness isn't measured according to our vision of reality nor our convenience. What answer can these nuns give if the discipline they've chosen is not to answer. The difficulty in understanding their life doesn't depend on the rigor of the Rule or the way in which they realize it. It depends on us—we who don't attempt to stop and ponder on the mystery of their experience.

It's not a new argument, but I don't want to argue this matter. Others have stated it with greater authority and, in any case, it's an argument that leads us far away. To India or beyond. When Saint Theresa, the effective founder of the Carmelite Order as it exists after the sixteenth century, relates that during her raptures in prayer it seems as though the soul is no longer in the body so that the body closes its natural heat and gradually becomes cold, she is merely indicating a kind of ecstasy similar to that of Indian mystics during meditation. The goal of Eastern practices appears then to be the same as Western mysticism. Annihilation of the self and oneness with God. It's the aim of psychology, Jung warns us, to ask such questions. Very well. I no longer remember who it was who said that there's nothing but personal madness. If everyone's mad, then everyone's sane. Well and good. Besides, what attracted me was, above all, the exterior—I'd even dare to say the visual—aspect of cloistered life. Which is to say, the Rule, of a rigorousness so stifling as to be almost absurd.

The thirst for suffering and humiliation that in earlier ages characterized the cloistered nunneries has disappeared. No nun nowadays plunges her face into excrement or washes the tongues of her sisters with rags used for cleaning the floor. The cloister has been modernized and nuns feel themselves to be women like other women. I put the question to one nun. She replied: "Certainly we're women like the rest. Virgin women, consecrated women, married women, women who are mothers . . . One gives birth in the spirit as well as in the flesh. The normal mother gives physical light to her child; the spiritual mother, if she's *really* that, gives her child another light, a light with no night, the light of God. I know this seems airy nonsense to you, but it's not. There's a way of loving that's pure and asks nothing for itself but wants only the good of another. Chastity is love of this sort."

Even when modernized, certain very harsh rules nonetheless persist. Like the rule of prayer in the night hours and fasting in the Easter season. And if a nun feels a need for flagellation or wearing sackcloth or a hair-shirt, she's free to do so. From what I've read and understood in my visits to fourteen cloistered convents, it's my impression that even individual friendships, which Saint Theresa called "melancholy matters," are tolerated if kept within discrete limits. In past centuries a nun who violated these limits, like someone found guilty of apostasy, was punished with prison. Today they're no longer imprisoned. It's mentioned in certain writings, but it's a vestige of the period between 1500 and 1700. Neither before nor after. Punitive methods are no longer applied. If a nun errs, the abbess will try to correct her by talking to her, and if the sister persists in her error she will pray for her, but it goes no further. They insist, that is, on love, on compassion, *misericordia*. The etymology is: *miseris cor dare*.[5]

Another rule still in effect is that no nun is permitted to make use of colors in her clothing or her bed. Or own her own things. When the prioress sees that a sister is attached to an object, she'll arrange to take it away from her. Once it was forbidden to touch, even innocently, a sister or enter her cell. The Rule required that everyone keep to herself. It was also forbidden to speak of the food one received in the refectory. In one of the nunneries I visited I lifted the napkin covering a nun's meal. Under it lay a tomato, a piece of bread, a slice of lemon, and an apple. It was a nunnery famed for its rigor, where silence is another of the rules, where mental prayer prevails over oral:

even the voice must be silent. Suffer or die, these should be our
desires, recommended Saint Theresa.

This long foreword represents the substance of an episode in
the diary, with which I wanted to begin my film. Thinking of its
realization, I've added a little color, but I've respected its au-
thenticity.

Again today I ask myself how I could ever have been attracted
by a theme of this sort. I believe I can say that it was the final
closing sentence of the episode that struck me. The glimmer
which that sentence stirs in the protagonist's mind lets him glimpse
an abyss from which rises, not, as some would have it, the sense
of eternity, but an earthly image. A garden enclosed by a very
high wall, useless flowers, pallid nuns, often ill, even though
filled with a joy that comes to them from the certainty of God's
love. And overhead the blue sky and the sun, like a monstrous
irony.

Christmas Eve. A rainy, fragrant evening. "Fragrant" isn't a
cinematic adjective, but I'm convinced that cinema can provide
even this sensation. That day the sun had set behind harmless-
looking clouds visible in the distance. Rain fell a little later,
slanting down against the walls. The smell was the smell of wet
plaster walls and asphalt.

A man comes down the steps of a handsome building, crosses
the courtyard, opens the main gate. He doesn't go out. He stands
there looking at the street and the sky. He's young, little more
than thirty. The day, nearly over now, is one that gave him
pleasure. A lively, stimulating day. A day full of imaginary telegrams, Fitzgerald[6] would say. Even the sound of footsteps behind
him is an event. He turns. It's a girl who with a smile asks him
to let her pass. The young man moves aside. The girl passes him
and starts down the sidewalk. She's wearing a raincoat that doesn't
show her figure, maybe it's a good one. She walks with a long,
even stride. She goes away noiselessly, as in a silent film. When
she was passing the young man, he'd tried to catch her eye but

he hadn't succeeded. He can't say that she avoided his gaze. She simply kept her eyes turned in another direction.

With the same naturalness she accepts his catching up with her. She doesn't quicken her pace, she makes no gesture of irritation. Not even when the young man, now at her side, addresses her. If she regarded him as a nuisance, a glance would make it clear. But there's no glance. That's the curious thing, she never looks at him. She has no need of being reassured by his face. It's not reassurance that this strange girl needs. A serenity that's almost indifference seems to pervade her wholly, a calm that spreads into the air around her, into the street. In fact, the young man no longer notices the rain, the smells. The conversation between them is just as quiet, including the question, "Where are you going?" The answer is: "To mass." "What time is it?" "A little before midnight." "Can we hurry?"—she says. As if it were implied that the young man were going to church with her.

There aren't many people in church, but the few there fill it with an unusual liveliness. They chatter while waiting for the ceremony to begin, they laugh, they exchange greetings from afar, with hasty visits among running children, muttering old women, and the coming and going of young people tanned from the ski slopes. The soundtrack is a subdued bustle punctuated by shrill notes that would make the needle of the VU meter of a tape recorder leap.

The girl takes a seat on an empty pew, apart. With a motion of her hand and a hasty glance, the first one, she's made her companion understand that she prefers to be alone, and she kneels. Throughout the entire mass she remains on her knees.

The young man isn't a churchgoer. He's not even a believer. He looks at that figure bent in the attitude of prayer, motionless, and waits for her to move. To turn. Any sign of interest would be a great pleasure. But the sign doesn't come. The young man gives up waiting, lets his mind wander. The people, the officiating priest, the pretentious and threadbare hangings, the voices of a choir without modulations. And then the unexpected silence. It's never felt natural to him to lower his eyes during the elevation of the Host. Aren't the chalice and the Host set out for the adoration of the faithful? And so why not look at them? But now it's not those objects that draw his attention but the girl again, still kneeling there, motionless. To him she seems even more motionless. Not to be deciphered. As though she were empty. An empty raincoat, the body discarded. This body of filth,[4] says Saint Theresa. Perhaps she's holding her breath? For such a long time? He tries imitating her. Thirty seconds, a minute, a minute and a half. He can't make it. She's dead.

But the spectacle of the girl absorbed in that long prostration of hers has touched him. He knows it from the blood beginning to beat in his veins. It's happened to him before with girls, when he's a little bit stoned on drugs, the same impulse to unite himself with them, to be one with them and at the same time to feel in the embrace a strange satisfying consciousness of his own existence. A kind of beatitude without passion, but extremely intense.

His mind wandered, evoking other moments, and the girl disappeared. The pew is empty. The young man springs to his feet, leaves the church. Everyone's there, very animated, they're in a hurry, they're hungry, no point in looking for the girl in this scene. His chest tightens with a desolate anxiety. He'd like to gnaw his fingers, letting her get away like this is idiotic. He doesn't even know her name. But he knows where she lives. He starts running.

The girl is slipping around a corner when he sees her. For the second time that night he catches up with her and she laughs. Her eyes are shining, as though she'd had a joint.

I'm going home, she says. She walks straight ahead, her pace is slow. The young man feels happy at her side. If someone told him that that girl wasn't made for the arms of any man, he'd laugh in his face.

The walk home is very brief. Suddenly there's the main gate. The girl stops and lifts her eyes, at last she too looks him straight in the eye. Only now does he notice her strong sensuous figure. It seems to him that he's never felt so intense a desire to possess a woman. But it's a different desire, with a certain tenderness and respect. It's ridiculous, he thinks. And yet there's a quaver in his voice, and he can't help it, when he says,

"Can I see you tomorrow?"

She keeps on smiling in the few seconds of silence that precede her reply. And her voice is devoid of all emotion when she speaks.

"I'm entering a cloistered convent tomorrow."

What a stunning opening for a film. But for me it's a film that ends here.

The brawl

READING Borges, I run across a (literary) account of a melee between Moslems and Hindus that involves the protagonist of the story. A colossal melee, three thousand people coming to blows, according to Borges.

I recall another (authentic) account going back to the last night of 1963 in Rome. A hundred people who came to blows, nobody knew why.

Since it involved people who weren't political fanatics, the spark must have been of a very different sort, probably casual and commonplace. I have a notion that, when so many people are involved, it's not easy to identify the opponents and specify the real cause of the brawl. The cause disintegrates into numerous other causes, localized in very small areas.

I see them, those hotheads involved in a free-for-all without knowing why. They're motivated by a secret violence, with no need for reasons.

A film that ends at dawn in a Rome dirty and deserted.

Story of a love affair
that never existed

At the end of September, night on the plain comes swiftly. Day ends when the headlights unexpectedly flick on. A little earlier the sunset had spread a magical light over the brick walls, and it was the city's metaphysical moment. That was the hour when the women came out. In the cities of the Po Valley women were a category of reality. The men waited for twilight in order to see them. The men were greatly attached to money, they were crafty and lazy, with the rhythm of tedium If money made them restless, women soothed them. In the Po Valley men loved women with irony. At twilight they watched them walking by, and the women knew it. At night you saw groups of men standing on the sidewalks to talk. They were talking about women. Or money.

The film I had in mind dealt with a strange story between a man and a woman in Ferrara. Strange to those who aren't natives of this city. Only a citizen of Ferrara can understand a relationship that lasted eleven years without ever existing.

My first idea of this film was different from the one I'm about to relate. A friend had suggested it to me on one of those nights that end up in the small hours at a streetcorner, chatting. It was a famous corner, where Via Savanarola meets Via Praisolo. Over our heads was a commemorative inscription: "Here, wounded in an ambush at night, fell Ercole di Tito Strozzi, most distinguished poet and philologist. 1508." Another story, this one too.

The protagonist of my friend's story was a young man who was in love with a girl, but the girl didn't return his love. Not that she didn't like the young man. Quite the opposite. Instinct made her say No. The young man nonetheless continued to pay court to her, and went on stubbornly doing so for years. Everybody in the city knew, and they followed the course of their affair and talked about it. But the girl persisted in her refusal. Until one fine day she yielded. The young man carried her away to his *garçonnière*, undressed her and she let him. She'd become docile and gentle. He made ready to possess her. But at the very moment he was about to do it, she drew back, saying:

"I've beaten you."

She got dressed and, without adding another word, left.

With this ironically emphatic phrase, destined to remain famous in the chronicles of Ferrara's love affairs, the true story of these two strange lovers begins.

There were no meetings between them except for casual ones on the street. But for everyone she remained his girl, and he was her man. Both of them had other love affairs, other sweethearts, but neither of the two married. Above everything else, or at the bottom of it, there was this reciprocal abstract fidelity. Which lasted, I believe, all their lives.

When Giuseppe Raimondi's book, *Notizie dall' Emilia*, by chance came my way, I noted the similarity of one of his stories to that affair. And it was in this way, through professional habit of mine, that I thought of a third story combining elements of both. I wrote it down, borrowing even some of the words from Raimondi. In literature this is forbidden; in movies, no. Because in a script the words that aren't dialogue but describe states of mind and images don't count, they're put in provisionally to announce something else which is precisely cinema.

This was the first time I'd let myself be tempted by the past. The screen has always toyed with history. A few directors have succeeded in giving credibility to their visions of past times. Certainly Eisenstein and Kurosawa, or the Tarkovski or *Andrei Roublev* or the Straub of *Magdalena Bach* or the Rossellini of

La presa di potere di Luigi XIV or the Kubrick of *Space Odyssey*, in the first sequence. But here it was a matter of recent times, the memories were within reach. Above all, I was attracted by the idea of treating Ferrara according to an imaginative chronology, in which the events of one period were mingled with those of another. Because, for me, this is Ferrara.

It's almost five o'clock when Silvano enters the moviehouse. The moviehouse is in an old theater with green-tinted walls, covered with an old, shiny varnish that recalls the patina of bronzes. The film they're showing is a story of love and politics. Silvano likes political films, with or without love. He's been twice to *All the King's Men*. At the end of the first reel, the lights are turned on. Everyone looks around, Silvano too. A crisscrossing of curious and provocative glances. One of these excites Silvano, inviting him to reciprocate. It's an intent, mischievous look that, in the dead quiet of the intermission, has the hint of a summons. It comes from a face that doesn't conceal its years, more than thirty. The woman looks and lets herself be looked at. It's as though she were asking: Don't you remember?

Silvano confusedly remembers. But it was the time when everything was going his way, even the faces. And this face he can't manage to place. An extremely strong emotion sweeps over him when the room goes dark again. Too many fresh years have been added to that older year, one year of eleven years. Suddenly, the neoclassical profile of that obscure Ferrara girl has come back to him.

A November morning, on a little train, crossing the plain toward the lagoons, the districts where the sea turns putrid. A pitiful sun, like the workmen waiting for it, so they can extend the aqueduct. A station. A rented car. A road covered with mud. On the road a girl leading a bicycle comes toward him. Silvano stops the car so as not to splash the mud, and the girl turns and thanks him. A slow, serious voice.

The young man has taken lodgings in the town's tavern, updated into an eating place, and the girl's there when he comes down to eat. There are tables with tablecloths, others without. The workmen are sitting at the latter. They eat pumpkin seeds and drink while playing cards. The girl lets Silvano approach her and they start talking. Then after sitting silently for a long moment, they go out together. Even the moon does its bit in helping Silvano, a white moon which the haze diffuses like an opaque window. The two young people resume talking. He, to give a bit of information about himself; she, to tell him about her life as a schoolteacher and her poverty-stricken childhood. She's called Carmen, she's twenty-four. There's some sadness in their words, but not a great deal. It's pleasant to hold hands in the humid night and take each other seriously. The water in the lagoon is the color of iron. When he hears a gunshot, it means that the fish-poachers have been spotted and are being pursued.

The two young people kiss with great naturalness and resume talking. He's never met a person with whom it's so natural to open up, but he's never thought it possible with a woman. And she, that a man could have so much to say. In these parts people aren't talkative. In fact, when they go back to the inn, where she's taken a room too, they're silent as though they'd exhausted words. On the stairs he attempts a few joking remarks to break the romantic atmosphere that's developed. Or in order to prove his patience, which is also a trait of love. And when he asks the girl where her room is, she replies frankly, that last room on the right. And she goes off, tightening her coat at the waist, a gesture that makes her slenderer, more modest, already submissive. At the door she turns as though to say, I'll expect you. Silvano smiles at her from a distance.

And then he enters his room. He's happy, calm. He washes his face in the cold water and starts undressing. He isn't thinking of anything. In his present state of mind, not even he knows how much he's affected by that strong virile satisfaction the girl has given him. He opens the door several times to go to her room. And he keeps shutting it, thinking that it's too soon, that it's only fair to give her time, or that it's not masculine to reveal his impatience. His behavior has historical justifications. We need to remember the abulia of the city he comes from. Centuries of domination, above all papal domination.

Silvano stretches out on the bed and goes to sleep. The night passes swiftly. The next morning he gets up, goes down to the lobby. They tell him that the young lady is still asleep. Silvano thinks of flowers, but flowers don't grow in swamps. On the sideboard he sees a fruit-dish full of pears and tells the manager to send them to the young lady, with a note which he writes.

At that time Ferrara had a secret charm consisting of a careless, aristocratic way of offering itself to its inhabitants, only to them. The peasants gathered in the cathedral square every Monday to transact business. Vigorous three-way handshakes concluded the negotiations. The third hand was the middleman's. But they then disappeared for the rest of the week, leaving floating behind them the noise of quibbling, age-old lawsuits on which the lawyers grew fat. The lawyers were overworked. They were respected and feared. One of them acted as theater critic of the local newspaper and was included along with a few other professionals on the prefect's list of invitations. The prefect at that time was regarded as the first citizen and every now and then gave dances at the prefecture. It was a privilege to be invited. Every year the Regiment of the Knights of Florence organized the horse races, the final day was the Arabian horseback pageant. The Arabs came from Libya, at the time an Italian colony. They wore the white burnoose and were mounted on small white horses, brandishing scimitars in a great cloud of dust. There were also organized military reviews in which the aristocracy took part because they were for charity. Toward evening lower-class girls left the factories on bicycles, their skirts flying in the wind. Many girls, and beautiful. They looked beautiful because they were happy. They were happy because they were going to meet their boyfriends on the old city walls or even in the hemp fields beyond the walls. From the green hemp blossoms arose an aphrodisiac pollen that fell on the city, stupefying it. It stupefied even the fascists, foundering in an obscene debauch of a local variety, that is, vaguely Frondist.

I would have liked to deepen this theme, but my producers at the time were not of the same opinion. They had a liking for the young middle-class people who played tennis or roved the city in complicated treasure hunts, or along the Po with motor-boats and spent weekends both exotic and erotic in Isola Bianca in the middle of the river opposite Pontelagoscuro. At that point the river opened up and the island poked up, like a piece of jungle in the middle of our own local Amazon.

This was a period in which Fascism was showing a certain normalizing tendency and favored limited evasions, from white telephones in movies to popular dance halls, which flourished. Business flourished too. But artists were in short supply. A painter by the name of De Vincenzi devoted himself to a grand effort to interest the few intellectuals with landscapes of the city and its surroundings under a blue Gauguin sky strewn with pieces of polenta. The pieces of polenta were the clouds. Few people went to his shows. Art in Ferrara at that time was a thing of the past.

When Silvano sees young people of his own age going by with their tennis rackets, he looks at them enviously but also with an instinctive detachment that makes him promptly forget them. And also because he's in love with a girl but one whom he rarely sees. He goes right on being in love with this girl whom he's never possessed, either out of stupid pride or a cursed prudence or simply because he lacks the will. Or from folly, that quiet folly of his city. He hears talk of the girl. The space involved is a small provincial capital and information about Carmen is magnetically drawn to Silvano and vice versa. Tenderness, anxieties, jeal-ousy, annoyance—everything that expresses the shared life of a man and a woman, these two individual lovers live them all separately.

But gradually, according to the law of time and distance, the tension holding them together relaxes. Silvano goes to live in another city, Adria, for instance. Carmen keeps moving about

from one village to the next, where the school supervisor sends
her. She has a child, a boy who dies on her at the age of two.

The lights in the hall come back on. The movie's over. People
hurry to leave. Silvano waits for the woman at the entrance;
when he sees her he goes to meet her. Few words are needed.
It's as though they'd left each other a few days ago. No allusion
to the past. Suddenly, a great haste, an attribute of the present,
has seized them. They go immediately to her house. It's an old
ramshackle house, with poplars in front and under the poplars
some cafe tables. Inside, it's a man's house. So much so that
Silvano would immediately ask questions if he weren't checked
by the fear of seeming jealous. And so he limits himself to observing Carmen. The woman is better dressed, and this dis-
pleases him. He's always liked faded and threadbare dresses,
dresses that don't adorn, that add nothing and even subtract
from, the body underneath. The dress Carmen is wearing clings
closely to her sides, accentuating a certain tiredness in her face.

The green of the poplars enters by the window, bringing with
it a smell of dampness. Silvano and Carmen decide they're hungry and she prepares something. While they're eating the wind
picks up. A conversation between the poplars begins. But the
two of them are silent. Maybe they understand that if they started
speaking, their topics, their questions would take on an intolerable weight and different feelings: regret, resignation, disappointment, shame, rancor would take the place of the sweetness
now pervading them. A sweetness into which they feel themselves sinking as one sinks in tall grass. Carmen tells him about
a letter she's just received from one of her former lovers. An
extremely tender letter. And her eyes immediately go damp.
She looks at Silvano as though wanting to tell him, you're not,
or you never have been, like that. She holds out her hand to
him, which he takes, and then bursts out laughing. At herself perhaps, or at their two hands reaching out over a ham omelette.

The fact is that their story, strewn with so many meaningless
hours, is there with them, whether they're conscious of it or not.

To give a meaning to the hour they're now living would require an imagination neither possesses: to invent, one by one, all those minutes, the gestures, the words and the color of the walls and the trees outside the window and the brickwork of the front of the house.

But all Silvano can do is move a few steps toward the woman, behind her, and after an instant's hesitation, bend down to kiss her. Carmen raises her hand to restrain him. It's a hesitant movement that means just the opposite. But Silvano pulls back.

There's little left to tell. The moment Silvano chooses for leaving is one of the many that follows that attempt. A longer than usual absence by Carmen in the kitchen probably. Silvano goes back down the dark stairs, leaves the gate. He lifts his face to look at the empty window. Two men sitting at a cafe table in front of two dishes of vanilla ice cream turn to look at him. If it weren't for those two witnesses, and because of a woman's name, Malvina, that keeps coming up in their conversation, Silvano would go back inside. With all his strength he wants to. While he's walking away, he feels like an actor reciting a part that's been assigned to him.

The street he's taken is deserted, as all the streets of this city must have been at the time when Ercole Strozzi was stabbed to death. His body was discovered the next morning, wrapped in his cloak, stabbed twenty-two times, his hair torn out. Thirteen days earlier he had married Barbara Torelli, with whom he was living. Popular rumor blamed the crime on Duke Alfonso d'Este, who had been in love with la Torelli. But G. A. Barotti, in his *Historical Memoirs of the Men-of-Letters of Ferrara* (1772) advances the theory that the duke was jealous of his wife, Lucrezia Borgia. It's a fact that Pope Julius II, angered with Alfonso because of his alliance with France, inveighed against him in an audience with the Este ambassador, reproaching him among other things for the death of Strozzi.

But this, as I said earlier, is the story of another of Ferrara's love affairs.

You want a . . .

SHE knows perfectly well she's hurt him. To throw over a lover after six years of living together is no joke. And so she urges his friends to stick close to him, help him get through this rough time. Not a day goes by but they aren't swarming around him like crows. They telephone, ask to meet him, write him notes, they even send him flowers. It's the first time in his life he's received flowers. When she asks for news of her former lover, they reply that he's doing well and she can't tell whether they're telling the truth. She'd like to make sure herself, but her gesture might be interpreted by him as a change of heart and the result would be to reopen a closed door. But it's strange he doesn't show up. She begins to suspect his friends may have told him some story or other, perhaps that she betrayed him. She decides to seek out his son, who's seventeen. He's a frank, no-nonsense type, who suddenly interrupts her.

—Why are you looking for him? You want a fuck?

She half turns toward him. Out comes a harsh voice, not her own.

—Want a . . . ?

The boy leaves, slamming the door. And it's that sound that makes her realize with no possibility of doubt that her life has really changed, that she's starting over from scratch. That she's alone and she mustn't feel pity. That pity will be no help to her in life.

Four men at sea

THREE men, exhausted by their ordeal, by hunger and thirst, have reached the port of Coff in western New South Wales in Australia. They'd been adrift for six days, without food or water, on a yacht called *Irene*. The men stated that, while the yacht lay off Port Stephen, the engine unexpectedly died and they were prevented from making land by a stiff ocean wind. As though that weren't enough, they ended up in a gale that kept them literally dangling between life and death for a whole night. On the morning of April 29, 1969, the *Irene* found herself eight miles offshore, adrift on an ocean as white and slick as a sheet of nylon. The three men, exhausted, were sleeping below deck.

One of them was wakened with a start by strange noises coming from the deck. Someone was dragging something. There was a sudden violent blow from the direction of the hatchway, then silence. The man got up, reached the ladder, tried to lift the hatch. The hatch door was shut from the outside. He then woke his mates and all together, with great effort, they managed to force the hatch. But there, waiting for them in the opening of the door, profiled against the sky, was the boat's owner, armed with an iron bar. Threatening them with this bar, the man harried them back down and fastened the hatch securely. A few hours later, after they'd once more forced the hatch off its hinges, the three men were able to climb back on deck, but the man had disappeared.

The survivors, including the seventy-year-old Charles Newlin, told of having been hired for a ten-day cruise by the yacht's owner, a Mr. James Towers, a rich businessman from Sydney, in his fifties. Twice in the course of the article, which I'm summarizing here, the newspaper advances an explanation, which is that Towers, in a sudden fit of madness, had thrown himself into the ocean. I don't believe it.

To begin with, I don't believe the tale about hunger and thirst. You don't start out on a cruise, not even a short one, without a supply of emergency rations and water or without Very lights. Towers might have thrown everything overboard, and in that case the hypothesis of madness would have some foundation. But the only witnesses of this madness would be the crew. The only opportunity they would have had of seeing him face to face was when the hatch was opened and they found themselves confronted with that wild man with the iron bar. Couldn't they, in those few brief moments, have mistaken a simple case of rage for madness?

Second, I don't believe that a seventy-year-old man would ever have been hired as part of an ordinary crew. If Towers hired him, he certainly had extranautical motives.

Besides, I don't believe that those three men, riffraff though they were, not only couldn't repair a broken-down engine but couldn't even send an S.O.S. That stretch of the Pacific called the Tasman Sea is crossed by the great trade routes to the Indian Ocean; a few ships would have received the message, they would have come to the rescue.

Finally, I don't believe that a man who owns a boat like that, a fifty-foot ocean-going cabin cruiser, a fast boat which handles nicely, on which he spends the most carefree hours of his life, a man who loves the sea—I don't believe that a man like that who wants to die chooses the ocean as his means of dying. A man like that knows that in death at sea there's an instant when the whole world takes on the color of the wave that smacks you in the face and smothers you. And he knows that at that instant he'll hate the ocean. No, that isn't the feeling a man like that chooses to die with.

Yet the mystery remains. And perhaps that's as it should be. Any explanation would be less interesting than the mystery itself. Still, this story has gone on working inside me for years. In its time, that is in mine, I had a passion for Conrad. When I read the story of the *Irene*, it was precisely this Conradian atmosphere of the open sea, of men brutalized or saddened by life, but who still retained a clean idea of life, that tempted me. So much so that at a certain point I decided to grapple with it as a subject for a film. A homage to Conrad as it were. At that time I was in Singapore waiting for somebody. For a director waiting is habitual. I wrote to the Sydney *Morning Herald*, asking if by chance they had any further news of the event and the people involved, or if they could procure it. The newspaper's reply closed by saying: "It is unfortunately impossible to satisfy your request for the simple reason that we are not equipped to handle investigations of this kind. Perhaps the Australian government offices in Singapore can put you in touch with a private detective."

Instead, I got in touch with an Australian acquaintance of mine and one month later I received a letter from him. The letter was unsatisfying but helpful, if for no other reason than that it enclosed a photograph of the three survivors, uncovered in the files of a photographic agency in Coff.

Here's what I deduced and thought after reading the letter and working out a physiognomic interpretation of the photo.

James Towers is a highly respected man, hard-working, correct in his business dealings. On this all the information tallies. On the basis of a carefree youth, he's built a quiet, middle-class adult existence. Rich, it seems he doesn't like being rich. Poor, so far as physical exuberance is concerned. He has no family but he does have the mystique of family. His release is the sea. The boat is the mise-en-scène of his manhood.

It's common belief that the problem of life is posed when something in your life goes badly. But that's not always so. It can happen that a man poses the problem when everything's going swimmingly and he suddenly notices that the stimulus of opposition, of an obstacle, is wanting. That's Towers' case. He wakes up one fine morning and feels the world around him completely lifeless. Stale. Sterile. And suddenly he has a yearning for the ocean. The day before, as luck would have it, he'd discharged his three-man crew. It's this obstacle that provides him with a fresh stimulus. He runs to the dockside but he doesn't apply to the usual agency for hiring crews. At the agency you find the regulars, the pick of the profession. Instead, Towers goes wandering the dockside slums and he spots three individuals who look like anything but sailors.

Conrad was right, you're either a sailor or you're not. But he was right seventy years ago. Things nowadays are not so clear, and problems of this sort, like taking on a crew, are resolved more on the basis of economic considerations than expertise. On the other hand, it's certainly not clarity that Towers goes looking for in the slums of Sydney. Quite the contrary, what he needs is a holiday from the rules, from respectability. And to him it seems that those three good-for-nothings are just what he wants.

Looking at the photograph, I imagine that, of the three, the tallest and oldest exercises a true and proper sway over the other two. He has an air of shrewdness, but not in the ordinary sense of the word. With his coarsely disillusioned and lordly look, he seems to have centuries behind him. A déclassé. An aristocrat of human misery. The man in the center is notable for a sardonic expression clearly deriving from his satisfaction at having survived god knows how many adventures. But also because of an alert mind, ready for any idea or enterprise. He's the strong man of the trio. A man who loves an effort when it serves no purpose. The third man is the slave of the other two, he'd die if he weren't able to serve them. Three men genuinely capable of anything, even of shaking with fear without being touched by the thought of death.

An hour later they're all cruising over a green sea, fresh and foaming. The morning passes swiftly. It's a new morning for

Towers. The talk, behavior, gestures, and expressions of his crew are utterly unlike anything he knows. The ability to make an experience out of this seems to him one of the strokes of good luck with which providence continues to shower him. The three men spend the time doing things devoid not only of nautical, but of common, sense. On the point of setting out, having sniffed out the man they were dealing with, they'd abruptly reneged on their bargain in order to demand better wages, exorbitant. Small-time blackmail that made Towers smile. The yacht's owner was too eager to put to sea with that trio not to give in. Unconsciously he was obeying a dictum by a writer—Samuel Smiles—whom Conrad had read and reread in his long ocean voyages: "The man who knows only reasonable or educated men, does not know Man, or only half-knows him." In fact to Towers it seems that the compensation in immorality and baseness he's getting from his fellow voyagers is so high, and that the mephitic air exuded by those three wretches mingles so well with the healthy ocean air, that he feels consoled and enlightened by it.

But he's underestimated the power of baseness and stupidity. He finds himself confronting both during the storm that breaks toward nightfall. In little more than half an hour, out of a seascape with a few low dark clouds lying on the horizon, rises a sky that becomes darker with every gust of wind. It's easy enough to imagine what happened during the course of the night. Towers shouts orders that nobody heeds and which are lost in the uproar of rain and wind. A powered yacht with its engines out of commission is a dead object, completely at the mercy of the waves. There's nothing to be done now except throw out sea anchors to keep the boat upright in the surges and ensure that its position doesn't shift. But it's an exhausting job for one man alone. And it doesn't even occur to the others to lend him a hand. The three members of the crew are no longer capable of being crew or even men. Unable to keep on their legs, they cling to any fixed object—railings, ropes, bollards. They have no fear, not in the ordinary sense of the word. Their blood pressure doesn't rise.

They're simply angry that the storm won't leave them be. All they can do is respond to Towers' orders with curses and insults. Against all reason, they even try to attack that man who's trying to save them. In this they're base and stupid. But they don't manage to reach him. And so their anger, exacerbated by his unreachability, merges with their ancient class impotence, and the yacht's owner becomes the symbol of human injustice.

At dawn the *Irene* is a corpse floating on a glassy sea, itself exhausted.

At this moment of sinister calm Towers must have felt the absurdity of the adventure he'd plunged into and sensed the danger he was running. The first thing he does is go forward to close the hatch, imprisoning the three men below deck. Then he goes to the control panel to check whether the rudder is working. It is. He glances at the engines, the breakdown is in the electrical system. Impossible to repair it with the few tools on board. But the radio's in fair condition. He's still examining it when he hears a hammering from below deck. Arming himself with an iron bar, he heads for the hatch. He gets there at the very moment when the trio is on the point of emerging. He forces them back down with his iron bar and closes the hatch as firmly as he can. He returns to the radio. He puts in an hour fixing it. When he's done, he lifts his gaze from the radio and looks out to sea. That's his relaxation, looking at the ocean, breathing it. At this moment then it seems the sea is looking at him and whispering something. But no. The whisper comes from the bow. He turns. Once again the trio has managed to wrench the hatch door off its hinges and is stepping out on deck. Towers stealthily circles around the bridge and hides. He's still holding the iron bar. Ocean, storms, lightning, cloudbursts don't frighten him. Men do. These men wouldn't hesitate for an instant to throw him to the sharks, later saying that he disappeared and in this way take possession of the boat, use her for some smuggling operation and then sink her. In the last four years two thousand pleasure craft have disappeared in the Pacific.

Meanwhile, the trio heads for the galley. It seems incredible that they don't see him. But they don't see him. They move

slowly, more exhausted by tension than fatigue. And it's fairly
easy for Towers to synchronize his movements with theirs. The
trio leaves the galley for the dining room, and they don't leave
there again until almost night to take possession of the owner's
cabin. Towers can then settle down below deck at the bow to
which the others no longer have any reason for returning. A few
hours later he comes out to get food and water, which he takes
from the refrigerator, replacing them with the same quantities.
He knows where to find the supplies.

He returns to the cabin at dawn, also in the nights following;
he sleeps during the day. During those hours, waiting for the
sky to lighten, a bitter melancholy comes over him. This boat
was something wholly his own, more his than his house in the
city; now it excludes him. Relegates him to a stowaway. It's a
role he doesn't know how to play. Also because he confusedly
feels that the trio that has usurped his place has some right over
the boat, if only because temporarily housed there and running
it. But what most astonishes him is that at the same time this
fact induces a state of mind quite new to him, a feeling of doubt.
A diffidence toward his own future as it were.

At times he's awakened by sounds made by the trio on deck.
He hears them talking, laughing, even running. One morning
out of curiosity, he lifts the hatchdoor, sees them drawing cush-
ions across the main deck and snoozing in the sun. They show
no anxiety. Whatever happens beyond that yacht seems to have
no interest for them whatever. They're indifferent even to him.
They haven't even looked for him. Why haven't they looked?
This question rises unanswered, leaving him with a feeling of
jealous indignation.

Every so often he notices sudden movement of the hull, overly
abrupt changes of course. A sign that somebody's clumsily handling the wheel, searching for a current. But it's as though these
operations, which for him would take precedence over everything, were for them secondary.

The shore is two hundred yards away. The boat has found a
strong current and lets itself be carried along. A few miles from

shore a fishing boat spotted her and took her in tow. From his cabin porthole Towers follows the berthing operation. It's twilight. A feeble and dubious light absentmindedly touches a port he doesn't recognize. A remote, dreary wharf.

And he's looking at this alien landscape when suddenly it seems to him that he understand one thing. He's spent his life giving too much weight to everything. And instead of taking fortune with a scornful smile, he's always been damnably serious. Only now, looking at that little crowd of onlookers gathered on the wharf around the three survivors, watching them enjoy what is surely the sole moment of glory in their lives, only now does that smile finally come to him.

It's night when he disembarks. The wharf is deserted. At the end of the wharf glows a motel sign. He heads for it and stops at the entrance, an aluminum and glass doorway through which can be glimpsed a squalid lobby, a desk, and an armchair in which a man is sleeping. No doubt the three men of the crew have also taken rooms in that place, they're in there now sleeping like logs. Towers looks at the lobby, the office desk, the telephone on the desk. He could telephone home, have a car sent to pick him up, or tell the man at the desk to get him one, or get plane and train schedules. He has no desire to do any of these things. He doesn't even want to sleep. But to step across the threshold of that motel—that he wants. To prolong for one night the life that he shares with those three, why not? He smiles, imagining their faces when they run into him before tomorrow. But he can't make up his mind to ring the bell. His habitual dignified reserve holds him there staring at the night-light in the lobby, a bluish neon diffusing a halo of intimations.

Where there aren't any houses

A flat expanse of landscape on the Po delta. A village of low, colored houses. The sidewalk continues beyond the end of the street. No more houses flanking it, only the sidewalk proceeding all by itself toward the embankment.

At night there's always a small empty truck, as though its owner lived there, where there aren't any houses.

That bowling alley on the Tiber

SEVERAL years ago I found myself in Rome, at loose ends. When I don't know what to do, I start looking at things. There's a technique for this too, or rather many techniques. I have my own. Which consists in working backward from a series of images to a state of affairs. Experience teaches me that when an institution has its own beauty, it's a good one. Why I don't know. Wittgenstein knew.

Well then, I was in Rome. I'd stopped my car on the Lungotevere in the area near the Olympic Village. I was looking for something I'd lost (I spend a good part of my time just looking). Raising my eyes, I saw a man emerge from the building that houses the bowling courts. His way of going to his car, of waiting before opening the door, of getting in, were odd. So I followed him. What follows here is the story of my imaginative construct of him.

A man leaves the bowling courts on the Lungotevere. No longer young, straight hair falling over his forehead, which he brushes back every now and then. He's a healthy man, you can see it in the color of his skin, which comes not from the sun but from the proper functioning of his own internal organs, as though the fresh air circulated inside him. His appearance is very important. What's about to happen to this man will happen only thanks to (or through the fault of) the self-confidence and geniality he exudes.

The man gets into his car, starts the motor, but doesn't leave. It's an expensive, well-built car, covered with dust and mud. The man's looking down at one of the pedals, he seems to be listening to the hum of the motor. In point of fact, he's looking at the tip of his right shoe where a scratch and a spot of red paint catch the eye. A spot and a line. According to the way the man moves his foot, the design becomes a line under a spot or a spot under a line. He must like the first pattern more since it's with his foot flexed in that position that he steps on the accelerator. The car drives a short distance down the Lungotevere and, where a side street enters, stops and yields to another car that's come up, then turns down the side street and, after crossing a stretch of very dark green, reaches the Olympic Village.

It's a strange day at the end of winter, no sun but bright, full of details. The man stops his car in front of a field blocked at the far end by a long, low building, with stunted horse chestnuts beside it. The man gets out of his car. The air smells clean and he breathes it in as though savoring it. He's not in the least concerned with breathing clean air, he has no hygienic conscience to placate. What strikes him in the place is a feeling that might be a feeling of peace if it weren't, depressingly, a feeling of inertia, of death. The front of the low building is all peeling away, the fixtures have turned black, even the grass in the field and the trees seem resigned to neglect.

On the field are two children playing. A boy and a girl. The man looks at them but not attentively. Or rather, he looks at them only when their game brings them before his eyes. But at that moment he looks at them with great intensity. The children come and go, fall, get up, laugh, shout. One of them falls somewhat clumsily, and the man smiles. It might not even be a smile, but the children think so, because of that geniality the man projects. They're probably thinking that he'd like to play the game with them, something that often happens, with adults, and they come forward to invite him. But something holds them back, perhaps the way they feel they're being looked at.

If someone asked—the boy, let's say—what will happen next,

what it is that disturbed him in the man's way of looking, the boy would have difficulty finding words to answer. Not ambivalence, anything but. The look was tender, loving, but a love so impassioned he'd never seen anything like it, not even in his parents' eyes. For this reason both of them hesitate to take the few steps separating them from the man. They stand there and wait, in a few seconds they'll return to their game. The girl has already made a movement suggestive of leaving. At the same moment the man puts his hand in his pocket, at which the girl stops, she's curious. She goes closer. But the boy stays where he is. Something inside him has clicked, a sudden, instinctive distrust, as if all the experience of his eight years had insinuated a suspicion of what was about to happen. The man draws a revolver from his pocket. The girl reaches out a hand toward the weapon, smiling, but not in time to touch it, and a shot hits her in the head. The movement of her body as it falls is of a strange and graceful slowness. The boy appears fascinated by it. An instant only. The man fires at him too and he too falls in the thick grass beside the girl.

The man puts the revolver back in his pocket, glances at the two bodies with a pitying look, and goes back to his car. He gets in, starts the motor, leaves. Without hurrying.

In one of the windows of the low building a woman appears. The woman looks toward the field, all she sees is an expensive mud-covered car driving slowly away. With a clear, still youthful voice, the woman calls out: "Olga! . . . Diego!" From the window she can't see the bodies of the two children hidden in the grass. The boy's body twitches imperceptibly. The woman goes on calling: "Olga! . . . Diego! . . . At least answer me!"

I know the story must end here, leaving the reader with the suggestion of that calm voice calling. But I feel a comment is required.

The preceding is only the embryo of a film, a narrative nucleus. To proceed from this, thanks to that technique I mentioned at the outset, to a more coherent structure isn't difficult, and, by so doing, satisfy all the questions the reader will ask: Why does this man kill, what's his background, what happens to him later and so on?

In Ferrara, where I was born, the winter fog moves in so thickly you can't see three feet away, and this was how, in my imagination, it happened. At a certain point one gets lost in the fog. I'll try to isolate, in this fog, a few firm points. First, the motive. Why does this man kill? I could reply to such a question by saying that it has no meaning, but already I'd be asserting something meaningful in response to the question itself. In short, if I had to make a film, I wouldn't ask myself why a film is self-sufficient and makes its answer through its own narration, in this case through the character of the man defined in his psychology or neurosis or madness.

But because this is a project doomed to end here, on this page, I can attempt a moral explanation, approximate and summative. This man kills to keep two innocent creatures from living a life he deems miserable, degraded, a life no better than a garbage dump. So his action is an act of love and at the same time an act of faith in something else. Paradoxical though it is, the idea at the time seemed to me not devoid of mystery and power of its own. If, viewed with more recent eyes, the mystery has diminished, the power seems to me have increased.

Another firm point. The man resumes his everyday life as if nothing had happened, in his own way, his conscience at peace. He's repeatedly been brushed by the investigations conducted into the crime, he doesn't lift a finger to avoid them. The detectives come to the door of his house, they open his door, look him in the face, but they don't identify him. They can't identify him. Because his crime fits so well into the social context in which it happens, because it's so normal, that is, among so many atrocious crimes, it becomes practically impossible to trace it, through its abnormal movement, back to the truth.

The rest is fog. I'm used to it. To the fogs that envelop our fantasies and the fog of Ferrara. Here, in winter, when the fog moved in, I liked walking the streets. It was the only moment when I could think I was somewhere else.

Tragic hunt

On December 13, 1975, forty-two people departed for a crocodile hunt on the island of Java. Twenty-eight men, fourteen women. They rented two boats and, loaded with provisions, proceeded along a river.

After reaching the place, a pool of water at the foot of a towering and sinister cliff, the crocodiles overturned their boats and they were all eaten, provisions included.

The girl, the crime . . .

WHAT most strikes me on entering are the eyes. I also like the position of her body, curved backward, one hip leaning against the counter, arms crossed over the chest, a long white hand on the forearm, motionless but set to move, to make gestures that wouldn't go unnoticed.

The eyes are bright but the look is dark, one of those dark looks that leap inside you and stay there. I can't help thinking of them in extreme close-up on a big screen. It's a commonplace shot but a shot of the commonplace is a permit that helps me proceed, it's a hypothesis of popularity. The eyes aren't really looking at me, but skim over me as though trying to see something that isn't there. A look that floats in that leisure time that hangs heavily over the shop.

The girl puts on a blue sailor's sweater. Almost everyone in town has this kind of sweater. It's a small town at the foot of a very green mountain, forming a semicircle around a tiny bay of white boats. The boutique is on the left, looking toward the sea. In the opening of the door the masts of the boats are seen swaying impatiently. There are two other girls in the shop, one less young, the proprietress perhaps, and another in obviously a subordinate post. All in blue.

The proprietress approaches me.

"Can I help you?"

Not only this sort of approach but the accent too are a little English. But it's an Italian *prego* that follows my answer:

"I'm just looking."

I go back to looking at that girl leaning against the counter.
She doesn't know I'm there for her. She almost doesn't know
I'm there. A worn-out raincoat entering a boutique is first of all
a raincoat. The man who wears it, unless he has special physical
endowments, goes unnoticed unless he buys. The girl doesn't
even remotely imagine that a mysterious circumstance could in
a few minutes seize her and hurl her out amidst an unfamiliar
and bewildering traffic. She's in the hands of that customer and
she doesn't know it. She gives me a sidelong glance without
interrupting her conversation with the other two, while I observe
her. I try to imagine the photogenic aspects of that face. Photogenic design has no rules. Usually a person with a broad forehead, eyes not too close together, a small nose and a jaw that
doesn't jut out does well. But the history of stardom is so full of
exceptions that it's doubtful this is a rule. Her voice is pleasant,
the lips move easily and don't show her gums when she smiles.
I immediately try dubbing her, adapting to her lip movements
a line in the script of a telephone call:

"I'm twenty-four and behind me there's a green awning. What
else do you want to know?"

All human behavior is learned, say the biologists. Inference:
Anyone can learn to act. This girl is acting already, they must
have suggested that her demeanor in the shop should be de-
tached and calm, that she should avoid any movement that might
distract the customer's concentration on the objects for sale. The
ideal clerk appears to belong to the customary order of the things
around her, she doesn't attract to herself the interest intended
for those objects. That she attracts mine is normal because it's
an aspect of my profession to observe people in the context of
the situations in which they exist. So I can occupy myself with
the girl without violating my role and without arousing suspicion.
I move through the shop in front of shirts and suits on hangers,
belts, wallets, ties, listening to the voices behind me. In the glass
doors of the display shelves covering one of the walls I see the

three girls reflected, mine in particular, from different angles according to the changes in my position. And since the clothing and colors in the showcase change, it's as though the girl were continually changing clothes and setting, and this proves useful to me.

Suddenly, the voices are interrupted. The proprietress goes out to meet a figure that stands with its back to the door, a woman perhaps. Slight noises come into the shop, then silence.

And in the silence I feel the presence of the girl distinctly growing. She hasn't moved, but she's turned her head and given a vague thought to me. And it's this I feel, her indolent vitality. Odd, that this is also the peculiar trait of the character in my script. She's a girl—the one in the script—quiet in appearance but vital, sensual. Someone who looks at her own arm while leaning it on an armrest or her stomach when she's putting on her nightgown, who touches and caresses herself, convinced of being the living image of an ideal love, of deserving it. But with the feeling at the back of her own mind that she shouldn't rely too much on this thought. Since the time she's been living by herself she does nothing but protect herself, but she couldn't say from whom. She notices confusedly that, even while loving them, men are her enemies and that by living with them she runs the risk of wasting away in a series of todays with no tomorrows. And so she's learned to regard her own fragility as the only reality in the world, the rest of it may be real or it may not (they're words in the script).

I think about these things while sitting in a cafe facing the bay, deserted in this season. I sat down as soon as I left the boutique, feigning a habit I don't have, in order to retrace in peace and quiet the course of events I have in mind. And meanwhile I let my eyes roam in search of stimulus from my surroundings and other combinations of events.

At 4 P.M. in this town the sun disappears. A little sunlight remains on the facades of the houses, poking out of the trees at the top of the mountain. Over the town falls a green light, ambiguous as the faces moving about. There's considerable irony on these faces, which attenuates their dramatic quality.

It's in this light and with no less ambiguousness that the girl plants herself in front of the cafe, perhaps a dozen feet away, without deigning to look at me. She stops to talk to a young man who's shown up with perfect timing, to give her the opportunity for that pause. Every so often she plucks her blue sweater, in no way affected by his vulgarity, even demonstrating it (perhaps). I have the impression that she's savoring herself with a sort of peaceful satisfaction at being looked at in a way she feels is unusual. But that she's ready to seize the occasion to transform that pause into a different, more active, more advantageous moment. It's not for nothing that she has that look of a girl with her head screwed on right. She doesn't want to be rude, that's why she takes time. Everything has to take place with great correctness, as they've taught her in the shop.

In the open air she looks even prettier. Unlike the young man with her, she's not tanned. Her skin is white, clean. If ever I could unite two such different phenomena as an image and a fragrance, I wouldn't hesitate to believe that she's fragrant too. But I've no more time for such considerations. The girl leaves her companion brusquely, interrupting him with a gesture, and goes to sit down beside me. For a few minutes she says not a word, she doesn't even seem to be waiting for me to break the silence. And, now that she's here and I know that a rite is about to be performed, I have no motive for hastening it. I restrict myself to waiting for everything to take place in a ritual way.

Instead, everything takes place in an utterly unexpected manner, beginning with the dialogue:

"It's better if I speak plainly to you," she says calmly, and her voice has a slight local accent that makes it explicit. Whatever you may suppose, I prefer telling you who I am."

"I prefer it too."

"I killed my father. I stabbed him twelve times."

The silence that follows is total. Everything is silent, outside of us and inside. Even inside her, I'm sure of it. She must have reconstructed the scene so often in her mind, each time sponging away, erasing, a little more of it. I turn to see the expression on her face. She's lifted her hand to push back her hair, then she joins her hands as though in prayer, gazing at two gulls gliding over the harbor. One seizes its prey, the other rests on the water.

"Why did you kill him?"

The girl shrugs her shoulders and her gesture, the movement of her breasts the gesture involves, is clearer than any answer.

"When?"

"A year ago."

"And you were acquitted."

"Yes. I did three months . . . and then the trial. They acquitted me."

I look at the sea which in the meantime has darkened with the shadow and I think:

"Stabbed him twelve times!"

But while thinking, I've spoken, and I add:

"You counted them?"

"They counted them."

"Where did it happen?"

She indicates the boutique with a gesture that stops in mid-air in that direction. She wants to be certain I've understood. It happened there.

"Generally it's bad conscience that leads to the scene of the crime," she says slowly, with a hint of sarcasm. "I went back there, and I practically live there, for the opposite reason."

She pauses very briefly, a movement of the erasing sponge.

"Are you going or staying? Would you like to see me tonight?"

Our meeting that evening added other things to the afternoon's meeting. Not the details, the information about movements, the mechanics of the event that I wanted to know.

"I don't remember" was her reply to my questions.

At dawn the next day I was again seated in the cafe in one of the chairs that wasn't dripping with dew. I'd come to that place to look for a character (attracted by a photo in a fashion magazine) and I'd found a story. And now this story let me think of nothing else, not even of my own. Twelve times she stabbed him. If she'd stabbed him only two or three times, I asked myself, would the difference between the real fact and the invented one be any less?

But this wasn't the answer I was looking for. The disturbing point was something else. It was that I felt twelve stabs were much more familiar, more domestic than two or three.

The first rays of the sun came from the sea to touch the chairs about six o'clock. And suddenly everything was clear to me, as were the sea, the houses around the bay, and the rest, in the sunlight. In that chilling number there was everything that there had to be in that story, there was truth. Not only the intrinsic truth of the crime, but also that of an outsider like myself, of anyone.

And one more thing was clear to me, that there was no longer any sense in staying on there in that place where the idea of a film had brought me and from which the same idea was sending me away. I couldn't have managed now to resume my own story except by telling myself lies. The girl's look of awareness, which had so struck me on entering the shop, had remained inside me and fixed me with tragic irony. The same irony I'd seen on the faces of people on the street, the same irony of the sunlight that was now touching everything, falling over everything like Joyce's snow, over all the living and the dead.

With this reverent thought of Joyce, I got up slowly and left. I was tired and irritated. As though I had just finished shooting the scene of the knifing and, instead of twelve blows, I'd decided that three were enough. Out of prudence.

The first days of spring

THE sensation I have when I feel that it's the shrilling of the telephone wires in the country that makes the landscape impatient. Especially in the first days of spring, when you hear more.

I think of this impatience transferred to people, peasant families for instance. It's not true that peasants are patient. And I think of the crisscrossing of the telegrams in those lines, with all their stories. And a soundtrack based on that shrilling . . .

Report about myself

I rarely think of my youth. I've never felt the temptation to make a film prompted by those years. Only once have I gone back to the memory of those days, indeed farther back. The projected film was entitled *Le allegre ragazze del 1924*,[8] but that was during my childhood, a somewhat colorless period in my life, except for that fact that, breaking with the norms of middle-class decorum then very much in evidence, I preferred to find friends among the children of the lower classes rather than those who, like me, belonged to the bourgeoisie. Perhaps I was unconsciously making contact with the popular background of my parents, who were, let's say, self-taught bourgeois.

Another occasion was several years ago, in a city that's not the city where I'm living now. I was walking by a florist's shop and I was about to go in and have some flowers sent, when a man about thirty feet away stops and raises his right arm to indicate something. I stop too in order to follow the line of his pointing finger, but I don't see anything worth pointing at. At that spot there are neither trees nor those high-tension wires of the sort one sees in the outskirts, there are no telephone poles, no trash barrels, no cars, buses, or people passing. The point is an empty passageway between two buildings, empty of everything but emptiness. The strange thing is this, that you don't have the sense that at that point the outskirts proper begin, as in fact they do. You have the feeling of emptiness. What the devil is that man pointing at?

He's about fifty, tall, sturdy, he stands there, legs apart, in
determined posture, and the beret on his head only accentuates
the threatening resolve of his tensed arm. Maybe he's a lunatic
escaped from the asylum; that happens every so often in these
parts. Or even a lunatic released on probation by the asylum
(*released* or *admitted* to another asylum?). Or, more simply, one
of those people who point to something that only they see, or
maybe that gesture escaped him without being ordered by his
brain. Nobody really knows how the brain functions, or how its
chemistry affects our behavior.

The building on the left of the passageway is low and at least
a century old. Its whitewash is a dirty white that becomes pink
in postcard sunsets. "We have thought often/The flaws of sun in
the late and driving weather/Pointed to one tree but it was not
so" (verses from a poem by MacLeish). That day, they pointed
to that building.

There's a shop, only one in the whole building, it looks to me
like a drugstore. All around the door and the window, about
three feet square, the wall is freshly painted, milk white, and so
the door, the window, and the piece of painted wall create a
white-on-white painting in the manner of Malevich.

A woman coming out opens the door and doesn't shut it. The
door swings a little and in the angle where it stops the man is
framed, and the man's finger at last finds its target. It finds me.
I notice it with a certain irritation, as if the man really wants to
point at me and not at the door instead, which by reflecting it,
reverses the direction of his gesture. The irritation leads me to
another thought. Why am I so interested in an individual who
behaves senselessly, controlled by who knows what urgings? I
have an immediate temptation to go and pull down this arm and
even to point it back at him, like the hose with which the day
laborer in *Arroseur arrosé*[9] is sprinkling a stretch of sidewalk.
And in fact I start toward him. But there are techniques for
resisting perverse notions. One of them is not to translate the
notion into action. That's what I do. But all the while keeping

my eyes on the man. His figure remains the sole focus of the entire landscape. Maybe he's one of those who come here every day at this time and raises his finger against—against what? Against the world, that is, the emptiness beyond the passageway. But this time there's something new in the scene, something else. I'm being accused. And the strange thing is that there's a vague sense of guilt at the back of my conscience, I feel it flowering like a shadow, a Hitchcock-like shadow of doubt that falls on the coherence of my life.

A girl goes by and asks me the time. I tell her and she looks at me with astonishment, and even a little resentfully, as though it were my fault that it's eight o'clock.

—Already?—she says.

She puts her hand on her forehead, slaps herself on the forehead, runs off and disappears. The incident serves at least to distract me and I turn to look at the florist's shop. The window is full of flowers that look wilted and also some of those thin, tapering vases, roughly six feet tall, of an earlier period. (I'd looked for them everywhere during the shooting of *Blow-up* to use in the sequence with the models, but there wasn't a one in London.)

From the shop comes the delicate sound of water trickling, a small fountain probably, mixed with the smell of flowers. Not a perfume, but the smell of wet leaves and stalks on the point of decaying. There's a feeling of death inside there. I look more closely, and I seem to be looking through the glass of those biers that hold the bodies of saints in certain churches. The spectacle is no less repulsive. I see some old people, very old, very thin and emaciated, sitting on green cane armchairs, talking. But their voices are the dripping of the fountain.

Hanging on a plastic hook on the glass of the door, I'd noticed a small sign posted. I thought at first that it indicated the shop's opening and closing hours, and now I see that it's a written notice: "The surviving members of the Fourth Levy will gather for a joyous reunion in a local restaurant on this coming Sunday at 6 P.M. Those born in 1882 are requested to appear at Bertini's

flowershop in Via del Convento not later than the day of the
12th."

A week earlier I'd returned from Paris where Roland Barthes
had told me of a rather disturbing fact that had created a vague
feeling of mental claustrophobia, like a feeling you can't escape
from. From the administration of the Collège de France where
he was giving his delightful lectures, he had been sent a list of
all the College's professors, arranged according to the date of
retirement. For one of them, extremely young, the retirement
date was 2006.

—For me it's the first time the twenty-first century has put
in an appearance—was Barthes' comment. And in his voice there
was all of his habitual irony, yet a little sadness too, which he
tried to hide as though the feelings were out of place.

I don't know why this incident came to my mind at that moment outside the florist's shop. I looked again at the notice of
the reunion and I suddenly felt squeezed, trapped between those
two dates: 1882 and 2006. And it was then that I thought of my
youth and I felt a crazy wish to make a film, a film about me,
that "third person" me of those years on which—rudely and
perhaps unreasonably—I'd turned my back.

It lasted an instant, that wish. And it couldn't have been so
irresistible if, as proved by the facts, that is, by speaking of it
now, it hasn't returned.

Untitled

FROM the river bank on up, there's an arrogant band of green dominating the landscape. Out of the green, on the right, emerges a red house and, above it, attached to the roof of the first house, another one, smaller, the color of brick. On the left a roof half hidden by the trees and a yellow facade. This facade gives the strange impression of resting on nothing.

I'm sure there's a story in that mass of volumes. There are stories everywhere, but the composition here is too unusual and the volumes are articulated in too secret a way not to hide something special. That space, between the houses on the right and those on the left, has to have the meaning of a fissure. Just as the nearness of the river has meaning. Those two rafts, their platforms deserted even in summer, and those canoes, slow when they move upstream from the sea, fast when they glide downstream with the current.

I like *to look out of the window, and see quite a different landscape* (Eliot, forgive me!).[10]

The landscape this morning is utterly different from yesterday's. The river is flooding. During the night the panorama was "rolled away." The yellow water drags away bushes and boughs. The trees crowding the bank give the feeling of no longer holding, before long they'll let themselves be uprooted, gently since the current isn't violent yet.

The windows of the houses on the right open at midday. Girls stand there looking. Those on the left remain shut. But there's something moving behind the slats of the shutters. I look with my binoculars. I'd say they were eyes peering. They remain there an instant and withdraw. Then they return and disappear again. As though it were a disagreeable sight, that muddy water full of tiny whirlpools sucking up everything passing nearby . . .

Toward the frontier

AT that time I slept very little; I'd adopted the habit of going to bed as soon as the day's gradual-fade-in began. Going to bed at dawn has at least this merit, that the day is well spent, sleeping. When you're not working, isn't this what matters?

I was in Merano sleeping off *The Trial of Maria Tarnowska*, a scenario with Luchino Visconti. Four exhausting months in a hotel room where Luchino kept us locked in. Guido Piovene, Antonio Pietrangeli, and I. In Merano I'd made three friends with whom I caught my breath, as it were, because they didn't think about anything. These three were a very young girl by the name of Sandra, from Udine; a German woman of twenty-four whom everyone called Grethe but Grethe wasn't her name; and an American captain of thirty-six. We had very little in common, but for us that little was a lot—the need for improvising our evenings and the feeling of bewildering brutishness that came over one in the small hours.

What I'm about to recount is the story of one of those evenings. It's lingered in my memory the way a film lingers, the sort of film I've always wanted to make and have never been able to, a mechanism not of facts but of moments that recount the hidden tensions of those facts, as blossoms reveal the tensions of a tree. I recount it because it was one of these evenings controlled by invisible looks. In short, an unexpressed tragedy. The characters in a tragedy, the places, the air one breathes—these are some-

times more fascinating that the tragedy itself, the moments preceding tragedy and those that follow it, when the action is firm
and speech falls silent. Tragic action itself makes me uneasy. It's
abnormal, excessive, shameless. It ought never to be performed
in the presence of witnesses. In both reality and fiction it excludes
me.

There are four of us in a jeep heading toward the frontier. The
jeep is going very fast. It's night. Headlights reveal houses with
wooden balconies full of geraniums and every now and then a
cross. For long stretches the road is rocky and dusty. Where the
asphalt's been worn away, rocks have poked up, a dry wind lifts
the dust and powders our hair. The captain is driving in silence.
The three of us are looking at the shadows fusing in the headlights. The gaiety of a little while ago has vanished, smothered
in a muteness that has no explanation, except that we're approaching the frontier, and frontiers always command a little
respect. They make us wary, especially at night.

Only when the jeep slows and stops in front of an isolated
house do we come alive. The entrance door is open, the inside
illuminated by a violently bright light.

"Gasthaus?" asks the captain.

"Gasthaus, ja!" answers a man at the door. Young, blond, very
young. Even in a language I don't know his tone rings false. It's
an answer that doesn't want to be an answer.

Grethe has jumped out. She has a wiry, supple body. You'd
say she spent hours at gymnastic or dancing exercises. The day
after I met her I thought I knew everything about her. I was
wrong. I went on being wrong even when our relations became
more intimate. Even now I'm probably wrong in describing her
like this.

I see her exchange glances with the blond young man and then
look around. There are other houses, none with lights on. She
looks at them as though listening. At the door, behind the young
man, an older man with dropping mustaches has shown up, fat,
enormous, a face irreparably scorched by the sun. He looks at

the captain who's started to enter but doesn't budge an inch.

"Excuse me?" says the captain. He has a thick American accent, the tone is emphatic. Neither of the men at the door moves. The captain looks at them in astonishment. His ability to be astonished by everything neutralizes the distance from which, as an American, he views us. Grethe steps forward and says something in German. The two men move aside.

Once inside Sandra starts laughing for no reason while wandering curiously about. She walks, swaying on her legs like a little girl in search of attention, but all she does is irritate. The blond young man comes up to her with a certain impatience and motions her toward a little room where the captain has already gone. I hear the latter saying in a loud voice:

"Eat . . . essen."

An intention of gaiety is evident in his tone of voice but it has the opposite effect. Grethe in fact becomes serious. Cheerfulness seldom assails her. She's very pretty when she's serious. Which often happens. She collects herself, retires into herself, or else comes out of herself. In short, she withdraws and then gives you the feeling she's no longer with you but in the company of some invisible person. The first time I saw her she was holding a bunch of flowers and suddenly she'd handed me one. I didn't know where to put it and told her so. I also remarked that mountain flowers have no smell.

"Flowers are more beautiful to look at than smell," she objects, and removes her gaze from me. She's succumbed to one of her moments.

Today, while I'm writing, an idea that occurred to me while observing her comes back to mind. A film, maybe. Born from the presentiment that I'd never see that girl again. But that, in some sense, she would remain in my memory all my life.

I know this is not a specifically cinematic subject, nonetheless I've always been obsessed by the idea of a film on the current that can be transmitted from one person to another, and that the latter carries within him, over the years. He's picked it up at the moment he's savored it, he's adapted himself to it, that is, he's let it become part of his personal situation and then, with the passage of time, he erases it. This is the absurdity, that no one takes pains to preserve his feelings, we throw everything away, and by so doing we gradually become the product of all the encounters we've had. But it's a product whose mathematical factors have been lost.

The dining room where we take our places has walls finished in natural wood, tables and chairs also of wood, a porcelain stove with a bench around it and a bunk over it. It's so typically Tyrolean that it makes one want to leave. The Tyrolean style suits Tyroleans only. But the captain seems at ease. He orders würst, ham, *speck*, beer, and dark bread. The blond young man writes down the order on a sheet of paper and disappears. I lean toward Grethe, who turns halfway to explain to me:

"This is Andrea Hofer's house. You know who Andrea Hofer was?"

I know. He was a Tyrolean patriot shot at Mantua after being informed on. I know another detail, that the informer's name was Schraffl and that this is the name of the proprietor of the Gasthaus. I don't know whether he, the fat man, our proprietor, is the descendant of that other sadly famous Schraffl. But he has the look of someone involved in the grief that, thanks to that name, ought to pervade the whole inn.

The house has aged well. The wooden interior goes with the bright outside walls, window sills crowded with the usual geraniums, sharply pitched roof, black, fused with the black of the sky.

The blond man reappears at the door. Grethe goes toward him and exchanges a few words. The man moves, Grethe after him, and I after her. Moves and opens a door. We enter a dark room. I hear the click of the light switch. Andrea Hofer, flag in hand, is there in a corner. It's a life-size statue of painted wood, so polished and shiny it seems to be made of wax, and being made of wax, it seems to be Andrea Hofer in person. On the walls faded prints: Hofer making a speech, Hofer at a clandestine meeting, Hofer facing a platoon of Napoleonic soldiers with blue uniforms and those long, long guns of theirs in a dreary barracks courtyard that recalls *Grand Illusion*. (One salvo wasn't enough to execute him it took twenty, so that Hofer commented, "How badly you shoot!") In the room there's also a table and on the table a register book for signatures. With the most natural of movements, Grethe hands me the pen and doesn't notice that I put it down where it was without signing. It's my personal protest against the blond young man whose regard for us feeds on such diffidence.

Meanwhile the young man has walked quickly toward the door. Before he shuts it, I catch a glimpse of two men, mountain backpacks stuffed full, going by. A third man, without a pack, follows them. And if the clothing and suntanned face of the last man betray his mountain origins, the other two have the pallor of city folk. I see them in the square of the window moving off, illuminated by the light at the entrance, stopping for a moment, then disappearing in the darkness. Behind me Hofer, flag in hand, falls. Grethe's at my side. I feel in her the same restless calm I feel. More to break the silence than from curiosity, I ask her:

"Smuggling?"

The young man takes care not to reply and scans me with a look bordering on impudence. His mocking air, as repository of all the world's who-gives-a-damn attitude, is intolerable, and I say to Grethe:

"Listen, tell your fellow countryman that the captain's an American and he doesn't give a bloody damn about what goes on here, and that I . . ."

She cuts me off. "He understands Italian perfectly."

"All the better."

I wanted to add that I too have an interest regarding that smuggling operation, that if he'll let me look, only look, then later if he'll have the kindness to show me the details, so much the better. At Merano I've heard talk of this trafficking in goods and maybe in men running from other men or the law. But I don't say anything. I haven't the slightest interest in a dialogue with him.

The door of the room is pushed from the outside, and the young man opens it. It's Sandra.

"This hovel must be a century old," she says impatiently, "but that's no reason why we have to wait another century to eat. I'm starved."

Grethe finally smiles and we all return to the dining room. In the meantime they've brought beer to a table. The captain fills the steins, lifts his own with a triumphant gesture, then lets it drop on the table. The stein doesn't break but the beer's splashed in every direction. The captain looks at us, happy as though he were only waiting for the fun to begin. But nothing begins. Sandra picks up a napkin and sets about cleaning up. She passes her bare arm several times in front of Grethe, and Grethe, with another of her more natural gestures, caresses it. It's an instinctive movement, tender and sensual at the same time, with a sensuality that seems to have a great sweetness of feeling behind it, like that of the three women in Bergman's *Ballo delle ingrate*.[11] A gesture so discreet it has no need to complete itself. In fact she doesn't have time for it. I don't know what mysterious presentiment induces Grethe to interrupt it a fraction of a second before sounds coming from the outside land on the table, making bottles and glasses rattle and startling all of us. The roar of a car's motor, or several cars, and a voice, or several voices shouting something, I don't know what—voices. I know that they're charged with a strange emotion.

The captain turns to look outside. He seems to be waiting for the noises to take effect. But the sounds have slipped away without leaving a trace and the silence goes back to being what a good silence ought to be, full of light sounds like the creaking of wood and the click of the pendulum. I look at the black of the window too, and I don't have the feeling that it's part of a night in the mountains, a night as full and solid as the mountains, an ancient, solemn night. But instead that it's been put there, that

black of the window, to hide who knows what movements, gestures, expressions, and thoughts we don't have the right to see
and understand.

"What's this place called?" asks the captain.

Grethe answers, "San Leonardo."

"My uncle's name is Leonardo too," says Sandra.

Grethe lays her head back, revealing her throat and asks for
something from the blond man behind her. The man answers
lackadaisically and she translates. (But why doesn't she start
speaking Italian when she knows he speaks it?)

"We're twenty miles from the border."

"Twenty miles . . . ," I start to say, thinking, "that's quite a
hike." As if she'd intuited my thought, Grethe explains that they
stop over in the Alpine huts and then cross where there's no
outposts.

Sandra starts making desultory gestures. "Pooh . . . but why?

She interrupts gestures and sentence. All eyes are on her.

". . . why are we talking about these things? Is the ham coming
or isn't it?"

A few minutes later the ham, the *speck*, the beer, the dark
bread are sitting in the middle of the table on two large platters.
The beer's strong, it goes to your head. Sandra closes her eyes,
gulps a mouthful, and puts a hand on her breast, waiting for the
hiccup.

"It's so pretty with all this foam . . ."

She sticks her finger into the mug, scoops up some of the foam,
lifts her finger to her lips and sucks it with a grimace of disgust.

". . . but I don't like it."

"And you like the wine?" says the captain. The idea of mixing
the beer with the wine takes his fancy. He laughs. He puts all
his effort into making believe that he's never in his life had such
a good time. But he's the only one who's enjoying himself. He
raises his glass against the light, inspects the tiny bubbles swiftly
evaporating, an indication that the wine's genuine. We all wait
for him to drop this glass also, but instead he gulps it down in
one long swallow, smacks his lips, pans his eyes over us with a

smile that has nothing to do with what he says, but which anticipates its banality:

"Boys, this is the life!"

From the way he says it, it's clear that he's not alluding to the wine but to our being there around the table at that moment, feeling good or feeling low, with those other men outside there in the mountains . . .

The silence now is deeper than before and lasts for some time.

"What are you thinking?"

It's Grethe's voice off screen. I turn.

"Grethe," I begin, in a whisper, "listen to me. Tonight we're extras. They're the main characters."

I point to the lobby.

"Why don't we resume our conversation?"

"What conversation?"

"In the jeep."

I take mental note of her leg leaning against mine. There's been no pressure on her part, merely a very pleasant warmth.

"But we didn't say a word."

She smiles, waiting for me to go on. But I'm involved in looking at the stove, at the majolica tiles with their blue arabesque patterns that break off where the tiles join, crossing the lines as though they were a border to resume in the next tile. I've noticed suddenly that I'm involved in smuggling too. Smuggling with Grethe, smuggling a feeling I don't have. But isn't this what we do every day of our lives, making a few of our feelings accessible to any event?

The dining room door creaks as it shuts. The blond young man has gone truculently off on his own. Footsteps are heard on the stairs, which are made of wood and echo. Again a tramping of feet, and the captain's voice imperiously shouting: "Open the door! Open it!"

The door stays shut. Then the captain leaps to his feet. He does so, one might say, willy-nilly, as though it were not in his character to leap like that. In three seconds he's in the lobby. But here he finds himself confronted by the fat man who irritably

motions him back. With an agility of which no one would suppose
him capable, the captain eludes him and plants himself in the
middle of the doorway, determined to stay there, entranced by
what meets his eyes. A woman's coming downstairs. Her head
is wrapped in a green kerchief, she's wearing dark pants, and
hiking boots. She's pale, her expression drawn.

"And who's she?" asks the captain.

The two Austrians pretend they haven't heard. The captain
puts his hands in his pocket, shifting the weight of his body onto
one foot, the stance of a man prepared to wait. Not that the two
men answer him, he knows they won't. But there's a change,
the entrance on the set of this new character has a certain effect.

The woman has stopped on the last step. It's obvious she's in
a hurry to leave and that half-drunk man standing between her
and the door is an obstacle that she doesn't know how to cope
with. She's not upset. She even seems to be thinking that, after
all, the matter isn't so serious. But it's become serious, that's
why she hesitates. Probably what disturbs the captain is precisely
the indulgent look with which she gratifies him and he reacts as
he can by appealing to all the *savoir faire* of which he's capable.
He makes a deep bow and says:

"Eine Dame zum plaisir."

The phrase sounds so weird in a man like him that it's unclear
whether it's an act of homage or a clumsy attempt at teasing that
keeps him bent over for so long, or even an instinctive feeling
of shame. However it may be, it's an uncomfortable position,
difficult to maintain. I exchange glances with Grethe. It's our
responsibility to go to his aid, or Sandra's, who's just appeared
at the dining room door. But none of us moves. Sandra, because
she's afraid of something she doesn't understand, Grethe and I
because, without saying so, we simply want the captain to fall
down so the woman can leave.

At this point, observing that he's losing ground, the captain
changes tactics. With the ability of people habituated to alcohol
to stand up completely sober, he turns in my direction and winks,
beckoning with an imperceptible nod of his head at the woman.

That is, he makes direct reference to me as an ally, forcing me
to reconsider the situation jointly with him. The woman, first of
all. Strange, that I didn't notice her beauty earlier. Maybe it's
her gaze, with that white makeup under her eyes, that puts her
features in such relief. And her erect posture, which forces me
to think of her again in a different way. What I don't understand
is why she submits to the captain's provocation. But nothing of
what's going through her mind is clear. From the way she looks
at us, it seems to me she intuits that all the forces against which
she's made her challenge tonight have united in us. We're the
norm, we're the law, conformity and so on, all the way up to the
supreme power. Or simply tiresome people. But for us she's the
unforeseen, the distraction. She's all we have to give a meaning,
as they say, to our evening. We can't let her escape. That's
certainly what the captain meant when he winked at me.

Grethe moves forward, halts behind me. I feel her eyes on
me like an invitation to intervene. Grethe's German and, as a
German, she's looking at me, boring into the nape of my neck.
I take the captain by the arm and nudge him toward the dining
room. He's become docile, I can entrust him to Sandra. When
I turn, the woman's talking with Grethe. Her voice gives the
feeling of colorlessness, as though she were trying not to be
noticed. Their conversation is short, oddly confidential. Without
more ado they say goodbye, shaking both hands like two old
friends.

Once the woman leaves, we all reassemble around the dining
room table. But things are not the way they were earlier. We,
we're no longer the way we were. The ham and the *speck* taste
differently. I ask Grethe what she was talking about with the
woman.

"She's in trouble," she says, serious. She has a face I never
tire of looking at. Everything in her is to be looked at. The one
thought that might take her away from where she is, that is, from
my gaze, is unbearable. That's why I start when (after a half hour)
she gets up.

"Let's be going," she says.

We pay and leave. The man with the mustaches accompanies us to the door, halting beside the blond young man who's reappeared with the look of someone who's never left. The captain looks squarely at them, with deliberate insolence.

What's the matter . . ." he starts out, in English. We push him into the jeep and I take the wheel. The two Austrians look at us from the threshold without a word, motionless. They're still there even when I back the car out and head for the road. I'm sure they followed the beam of our headlights moving over the trees and disappearing.

That the beam of the headlights leaves its mark on the trees when it illuminates them at night, I learned once when I aimed the car's headlights at an oak, and got out to look. The bark was swarming with ants coming and going with their customary stupid industry. Only the point touched by the headlights was empty of ants. The ants were scurrying around it, grazing the perimeter without once entering the circle. And they went on avoiding it even when, headlights switched off, the light disappeared from my sight. Not, it would seem, from theirs.

We drove a few miles and stopped. The captain has seen some trees loaded with apples on the embankment on one side of the road and wants to pick some. We climb silently up a slope but don't manage to reach the orchard which remains hidden by a clump of larches. We come to a clearing the same instant the moon pokes up and the grass turns green again. Two pounds of blue is bluer than one pound, Gauguin used to say. Nature has lavished tones of green here. We cross the clearing more out of a need for going on, for getting somewhere than anything else. In front of us is a wood that looks to be impenetrable. We move closer for a stretch until we reach an opening with a path leading off. We take the path. For a path in the middle of the woods, it's oddly straight, strangely precise, no more to be avoided than the innumerable trees looking at us indifferently, probably with hostility. The moon filters through the branches, making patches

of white and then black, and we move forward from light to
shadow, wary of making any noise, who knows why.

After a bit the captain and Sandra abandon the path with the
excuse that the apples are somewhere else. Grethe and I go on.
We'll meet at the jeep.

There's a sound of distant shots, their echo fills the valley,
leaving us with a vague sense of anxiety. Anxiety, not fear. Those
shots weren't aimed at us. If I had a rifle, I'd fire too, just to be
part of the enigmatic atmosphere of this night. At a certain moment Grethe takes me by the arm and points to a spot among
the foliage. We go closer. At the edge of another clearing, not
so wide as the first, are two figures, a man and a woman illuminated by the moonlight. I prefer daylight to moonlight, the
dazzling light of the sun to the moonlight, however suggestive.
But it also happens that people can be illuminated by moonlight
without the scene becoming idyllic. The scene would recall the
scene in *Blow-up* if time hadn't reversed the order of the two
events. At the time *Blow-up* was still to come. And anyway its
night would be a moonless one, lit by a neon sign. Here, however, an enormous, golden disk appeared. It seems to have been
setting instead of rising, to illuminate the event that's about to
take place.

During the last war, on a night like this, a man had killed a
German soldier in an Abruzzi village. I was hiding with two
friends in an attic, watching the piazza below through a chink.
There were people running away, others streaming toward the
house where the killing had occurred. I would have gladly paid
to go out. We'd been shut up inside there for a month to avoid
being deported and I was awake much of the night. I used to
look at the moon. I was trying to understand why that moon
aroused in me a negative feeling. There's something funereal,
or at least mysterious and anguished, in moonlight. We know
that the surface of this heavenly body is white, chalky white, and
that, seen close up, it's an image of perfect desolation. And we
know that, insofar as it's a heavenly body, the moon doesn't shine
with its own light but reflected light. What reaches us is only

the reflection of its desolation. Between us and the universe it interposes a fine bluish dust that intensifies the contrasts. Blackness becomes blacker, whereas white and the whole spectrum of pastels fuse in a single earthy pallor. Our faces become insubstantial and things that, during the day, seem to be alive with change, are fixed in a sorrowful immobility.

It's an alchemy that produces its own effects on human beings. That night in that Abruzzi village must have bewitched the man who'd killed the German, so little was needed to unleash his jealousy: a vague attempt to violate his daughter. Maybe it bewitched the German and the girl herself. They were embracing when the man came into the room. The German's machine gun was leaning there against the wall. The man seized it, caught up with the soldier on the stairs, and fired a burst at his head. The body rolled down to the door. Beyond the door there was a glimpse of the piazza illuminated by that "sepulchral torch" (Charles Fourier) that is the moon.

The woman in the middle of the clearing is the same woman the captain was trying to detain. I don't know the man. Wiry, sure of himself to judge from his gestures. We hear, barely audible, her voice and, after a pause, his. They're about thirty yards apart but they speak in a tone that in theatrical jargon is called "whispering," as though they were face to face. Their voices alternate without ever overlapping, but with perfect timing. I ask Grethe what they're saying.

"A few words, they're speaking so softly . . ."

A minute later I notice a different whispering, no longer in sync, like a sob. I look at Grethe, it's she, she's weeping. For the second time in the course of the evening her reaction precedes what happens an instant later. A shot of a firearm. It's closer than the earlier ones but I can't say it was the man who fired. This shot too dissipates in the valley below and the silence of the mountains buries it.

The woman's no longer where she was. The man's there, but he suddenly moves off. He takes an extremely long time to cross the level ground and he remains just as long looking from the other side at the spot where the woman was, where she maybe still is, lifeless. And then at the woods, at that point in the woods where the woman may have run. Both theories pass through my mind. Given my doubt, I should at least have tried to catch up with the unknown man, follow him. Why didn't I? Why did I stand still watching the clearing even when, after the man had vanished, there was nothing to look at?

I remember a flash of insight that came over me like a certainty. There was no reason in the world why we were in that place at that time. We were two useless witnesses and I instinctively rebelled by staying where I was.

I put an arm around Grethe's waist with no other thought than of comforting her (but from what?) and I guide her to the jeep. The others are already inside. Sandra's eating an apple as though it were morning. The captain's a bit dejected, his gaze is heavy, his eyes look like leaves in the wind (where did I read that phrase?). We leave, Grethe's knee touches mine again and that contact offers me such a tender complicity that I no longer want to return to Merano. I make a U-turn, reversing direction. The road starts going downhill and I turn off the ignition. I also turn off the headlights. Now we're sliding along the wavering white of the road, toward the frontier, listening to the gravel softly crunching under the wheels in the silence.

Out of desperation

WITHOUT a word a girl sits down at my table in a bar in Piazza Bologna in Rome. She's extremely excited. She tells me she's just witnessed a kidnapping. Two young men in plain view grab a man and shove him into a car which drives off at great speed. They're armed and nobody can do a thing.

The girl has beautiful dark eyes and a strange way of looking. Looks like rustlings. She says she's a maid in the house of an old lady, a former history teacher. Her life is lived in the same way as that seventy-year-old woman. Her world is there in the windowpanes, and every afternoon the girl goes out and wanders through her world, which is the neighborhood where she lives. When she comes back home, her mistress is sleeping and out of desperation she starts reading the history of Italy.

On the street one day she stops to talk with a boy of her own age. He's not a talker. She likes him. Shyly the boy tells her of his interest in her. And there she is. And she falls into the net of her destiny—terrorism, underground existence, prison, escape . . .

Out of desperation.

The desert of money

IN a very beautiful spot, in the green growth, I discover a dead man's body. Walking through tall grass, I almost stumble on this body. A suicide, they'll declare later. It's not the first time I've seen a dead man, but previously I'd always felt grief, or else indifference. Confronting this corpse, I feel neither, I feel something different. He's a dead man who preserves an extraordinary charge of life. I seem to feel his blood pulsing, to intuit his thoughts, the tumult which led him to take that action. He's close to me, this dead man, as he never would have been when he was alive.

Clearly he's not been dead long. The skin isn't yet transparent. If I ever have to suggest to an actor how to play dead, I'll know now how to describe it. The dead man's stretched out on his side, right hand lying loosely on his neck, the pistol half hidden in the grass as though he'd let it drop the very instant he pressed the trigger, a useless change of mind. You'd say that nothing in this man has changed. He's merely pased from one state to another, quite naturally. There's a small hole in the right temple, neat and clean, not a drop of blood has oozed from that hole. His eyes are open, an indication he wanted to die looking. But looking at what? A line projected from his eyes leads directly to a bush of yellow crategus; behind the bush rise some elms; between the elms a house, a bit of pink facade with a dark window in the middle. We're on the outskirts, be-

yond that house the city proper beings—Bologna. The sounds
of the city don't reach this place. But sounds, voices, noises
are very distinctly heard coming from that house, or from
the room, whose window is open. Who live in that house?
To die looking at a window, with perhaps a woman standing
in it, to die at that precise moment looking at that woman
who will have heard a bang in the distance and thought nothing
of it.

No, this isn't a love story. This is a story about money. I've
always had a great curiosity about money. Curiosity, not interest.
When I was getting ready to shoot *L'eclisse*, I saw tens of billions
of lire vanish in a few hours into thin air in the Stock Exchange,
where there's always a loser but maybe no winners. In Las Vegas
I saw a woman spend an entire afternoon in front of a slot machine, and when finally the machine dumped out a pile of half-
dollars the woman went off without scooping them up. She was
a woman who looked directly at nobody. I'd have liked to talk
to her, but in Las Vegas words don't count for much. They count
a great deal here in Italy, sometimes more than money. And it's
a peculiarity of my profession to know how to speak to people,
to make them talk, to become their accomplices in this need of
theirs to confide, to tell their stories as protagonists in whatever
desperate situation.

Well, I went into that house, I went to the window: the
dead man had been carried off and the meadow was deserted,
strange birds were flying over. At my side was a girl of
about twenty-four, the younger of the two women I met in
my inquiry. Along with the dead man, they're the characters
of this report or story, since I had to treat the material I'd
gathered with the thought of making a film from it. It's
material that becomes a burden if the film isn't made, I write
to free myself from it. Hence I'm a director who writes, not a
writer.

This time the characters struck me more than the story. Their
squalor, their animality, their childishness, their lack of intelligence in living. But also their absolute coherence, this makes

them disconcerting and moving at the same time. Their names are Emma, Oriella, Leonardo.

Emma. Thirty-six years old. Regular features, pretty. On her husband's death she went into business, taking advantage of his circle of acquaintances. She doesn't give the impression of being a greedy woman but, if so, she seems to amuse herself by being so. With her informal air, she puts men at ease, more so than women. She knows how to be provocative and broad-minded, above all she's tolerant of other people's broad-mindedness. She frequents nightclubs, discos somewhat less; in one nightclub she met Leonardo. She dances very well and, while dancing, talks about sums of money, promissory notes, contracts, which she later signs with a kind of indecipherable hieroglyph. She lets people think anything—that she's honest, that she's not—she lets them think either as she finds it convenient. But if they talk about family or children, she's moved, that's what she wants more than anything else, a family, peace and quiet. But only in words is this true. In actuality, from the moment she entered the world of small finance, a partition went up between her and the other world where family's the normal thing. Her very life-mechanism excludes it, this normality. She's awake by nine in the morning and she doesn't stop until the small hours. Her day runs with the rhythm of her appointments. She plans many deals, but if they can't be settled promptly, she abandons them. Usually she settles things by arguing them out with the other inter-ested parties, but it's not so much a matter of settling things as of a true and proper illumination of poetic quality, that *involuntary* poetry that Paul Éluard opposes to *intentional poetry*.

She eats very little and very well. She also dresses well, with middle-class taste, but seems not to care about it. It's not true, she cares a great deal about herself. One might say that she thinks only and constantly of herself, in the sense that she has a constant need to feel alive, shut up in her cell as she is, the way it must be for a baby in its uterine life. She's constructed a world wholly for herself, she herself is a world unto heself. To enter there is a privilege.

Oriella. I think the dead man never enjoyed this privilege. That the problem was never posed. Problems are what a secretary is for. It's almost with a sense of guilt that Oriella accepts this designation. She's neither efficient nor attractive, she knows it. She likes to talk and this, in the ups and downs of their relationship, is her strong point. Above all, she says things that he never thinks about. For instance:

"You know that once, millions of years ago, scorpions used to live in the sea?"

Oriella also knows a little English. She takes Berlitz lessons. One morning she comes into the office and announces that yesterday evening she learned a word that's suited to money: *zest.*

"What's it mean?" Leonardo asks.

It means taste, savor, aroma, in the sense of "fizzy," also. Here's still another of those matters he's never dreamt of thinking about, that money can have a savor, an aroma. For a man like him, who lives on money, who buys and sells it, it's the only merchandise for which there's always a demand. It's a discovery, he says.

Oriella is jealous of Leonardo. The man's relationship with Emma has such power of inertia that it's prolonged over the entire length of their separations. Practically, Emma's always there, in the office. A promissory note she's signed, a draft she's drawn, a check made out to her, an I.O.U. she's initialled— they're all occasions for introducing Emma's name in their conversations. The girl doesn't know her, has never seen her. Emma's always managed to avoid her. Maybe that's why Oriella is so curious about her, asks questions, wants to know. She wants him to explain the sexual difference between them, which has the bigger clit and whether Emma talks during orgasm and what she says.

When I asked her what she found attractive about that man, she gave me two answers instead of one.

"He's very virile," she says. And nothing else. But a little later she thinks it over, as though remembering, and adds: "And then he's honest. He'd learned to be honest by handling money. With money you can't tell lies. Money will reveal the truth right away.

What I find most striking about her is her logic, her concreteness. With her absentminded and insubstantial appearance, it's the one thing she's grasped on her own, her limits, and to have adapted her ambitions to those limits, her behavior with the man to her ambitions. She's tried to love him and she's succeeded. She tried to make him love her, but his death upset the idea she'd developed on this score.

"I made a big mistake," she says, "when I refused to take money the last time he dumped me. That was when my stocks went down. You don't ever refuse money."

Leonardo offered it to her as a separation bonus, her refusal irritates him since it means that his accounting is wrong, he feels he's in debt. He doesn't like being in debt. From his father he's inherited a handsome capital—honesty.

Leonardo. To every question Oriella asks him he replies in a kindly, condescending tone. He doesn't reckon that it's he who's being rewarded since those questions give him much greater pleasure than his answers give her. As when a mother bathes her baby boy and the boy screams when she washes his face but quiets down the minute the sponge reaches the bottom of his stomach, between his legs. It's a masturbation unconsciously performed by the mother and which in her is identified with love. This pleasure Leonardo takes in listening to Oriella talk is his love for her. He doesn't know how to give her anything else, and he doesn't even know how to give her this. He doesn't know anything, he doesn't understand anything. He *does*. And he does more and better when he's by himself, or in the lulls between one affair and another. And since doing for him means earning, he earns more. He succeeds in achieving greater concentration. He shuts himself in his room, slips into bed even in full daylight and thinks. Of business. In that moment he's starting up a well-oiled mechanism, fueled by innate cunning and an experience accumulated over the years. In an hour or so he's resolved it. As one resolves a problem, going from one equation to the next.

But Emma's presence forces him to adopt a different technique, a joint effort to which he's unaccustomed. Also because she's not endowed as he is with that hard sixth sense so useful in business. Money flourishes in scorched lands, in those spiritual deserts where there's not even a grain of sand, because sand conceals unanticipated reserves of life which one night's rain is enough to get sprouting. I was present at one of these spectacles. There was a thunderstorm at night and the next day I woke up to see the desert spotted with lilies. Magnificent. But deserts of money are deserts of stones polished smooth by an implacable wind. Thoughts, emotions, amusements—it blows them all away.

These are the characters. The factual mechanics have the simplicity of a theorem in geometry. The initial situation is one typical of the businessman who hires a secretary and becomes her lover. When, a year later, he meets another woman and in his own way falls in love with her, he breaks with the first. It's the woman herself who asks him to do it.

"I don't want to cause trouble," she says, "but does it seem fair to you to keep your ex in the office?"

This first segment of their story isn't long. I pass over the reasons for the friction which leads to their separation, a business deal gone sour, I suppose. I know that when it happens he turns to Oriella for refuge in search of consolation or company, or merely the sound of her voice. And, practical man that he is, he restores her to her place in the office. The second segment is longer. The third, extremely long. Each time he pays the girl off with a sum that increases in accordance with the devaluation of money. It's ridiculous, this emotional and monetary fluctuation. On the other hand, every reconciliation with Emma is accompanied by the prospect of a large investment of money, proposed by her. What else can he do? Renouncing her is the last thing that enters his mind.

The last enterprise is risky and requires an exhausting argument on what line to take. The deal comes off. Both of them, pleased and satisfied by the profit they've made, believe they're happy. On the way home they decide to spend the night in a famous vacation resort. But it's winter. Completely closed, colorless, the sea white and foaming, the pavement wet, the branches naked. An atmosphere as commmonplace as the clouds scurrying over their heads. They remain for a few minutes staring at a summer awning lashed against the window by the wind, listening to the clattering of its rings against the glass. The awning's reflected when it approaches the glass; blown back, it disappears. They end up in a nightclub where they're trying out the programs for the summer season. There's an Iranian singing a torch song about letters that were never received—"I've written you letters too . . . letters filled with my tears . . . the tears are in my letters, dear."

Suddenly Emma starts weeping. He looks at her, he feels no sorrow, no pain. On their return to the hotel, they're both so depressed that they believe they're unhappy. And maybe they are. They divide their profits, signing two checks, and separate.

Oriella cites me a curious detail. Immediately after leaving Emma, Leonardo went as usual to Oriella. He finds her cold and distant. There's no conversation. It's a day of sunlight and rain. When they parted in the street they shook hands, that is, they extended their hands but without touching. Oriella says she wasn't looking at him but at those two unjoined hands wet with rain.

When the man is finally left alone, with that money which no longer smells of anything, he's truly alone at last. Too alone.

Neither in heaven
nor on earth

THIS idea is set in an unspecified spot. Any reference to reality is accidental.

Protagonist, a physicist. A man familiar with a muon, an andron, a lepton, who can define their meanings by quantifications. Extremely advanced in the study of invisible reality, he's distressingly backward in relation to visible, that is, everyday reality. He's as open and penetrating in the scientific field as he is narrow and banal in more ordinary subjects, especially those closely affecting his family and the community of which he's part. This community is limited to a circle of a few miles, and he lives there, keeping up sporadic contact with the outside world. In little villas, all very ornamental, built around a cyclotron, whose nourishment is microphysical concepts and clichés, scientific breakthroughs bordering on poetry and bourgeois stupidity.

The workers and peasants who live in the area surrounding the cyclotron look at him and his colleagues as though they were unknown animals. What most astonishes them is that these scientists speak the same simple, practical language, and use the same words to speak of things that exist neither in heaven nor on earth.

A pack of lies

THERE are five of them on the trip.

A professor, his wife, an anthropologist friend and his mistress, a doctor. The trip will be long and dangerous. As it turns out to be, typical of a mentality which among us is generically termed bourgeois.

One day the anthropologist tells the professor that his mistress is in love with him. Uneasiness of the professor, who's very faithful to his wife and wants no deceptions. He asks if the others know. Yes, they know. His wife too? His wife too. His mistress herself told her. She's told everyone except him. It's an old, stupid custom that a woman in love doesn't reveal her feelings to the person who's their object. But his wife, at least at the level of amused complicity, might have told him.

Is a truth untold a lie? It's possible. But the professor is careful not to reproach his friend's mistress. Certain lies are useful, others harmful. It would be a real godsend if he could introduce a little jealousy into his relationship with his wife. So the professor limits himself to making a single condition for continuing the journey, that the mistress and everyone else behave as though nothing had changed. No drama, arguments, recriminations. No gossip.

This is what happens. But from that moment on all naturalness in the relationships of the five travelers vanishes. No apparent embarrassment. Merely as greater courtesy in their encounters, extreme attentiveness. Graduallly they're all trapped in such a web of falsity that the very reason for the trip collapses. Four of them have agreed to stop the trip. Not the professor. The new situation serves his purpose and it gives him a euphoria he hasn't felt for years. He wakes up in the morning with this thought in mind: another woman has entered his life. Nothing comes of the thought but it gives a savor to his day.

All this lasts until his wife announces a new fact. The woman in love with him has suddenly fallen for the doctor. Nobody in the group is aware of it. The confession, the wife says, was made only to her in order to relieve her, and she seems utterly sincere. But this is a lie too. A little conjugal trick designed to accomplish two ends, to deter her husband from a possible affair and to conceal another incipient affair between her and the anthropologist's mistress. The violation of conjugal trust with someone of the same sex is no longer an act of adultery, it's the dialectical conquest of a political space. And it causes no remorse. To the two women, it seems that they're traveling in a dream. To the husband, a colorless steppe with no horizon. He feels cheated, made ridiculous in his wife's eyes and in his own, so much so that in the last few days he'd cherished a secret thought of passing on that story. And he has nobody to whom he can confide his bitterness. Friendship would suggest the anthropologist, but it's precisely he who mustn't be told the truth.

And so the trip, and the film, proceeds in this atmosphere of double and triple falsehood. The five travelers pass through lush landscapes (Peru, let's say), prairies falling away toward the sun at twilight, dark forests marvelously full of birds, waterfalls, and gorges that they don't see. Even with nature they lie.

Title in Italian: *Un mucchio di bugie*. For the English-speaking market: *A Pack of Lies*.

They've murdered a man

THEY'VE murdered a man at Ferrara by making his car plunge into a branch of the Po. In winter, with the fog veiling the countryside. The car was under water all night, headlights burning.[12]

The story of this man summed up in this, his final moment, tells us little. Something else has to happen in that place, in the course of that same night, in the glare of those headlights under water. That watery light beating on the fog as on a window of frosted glass is too suggestive not to be utilized. And then there's novelty in a narrative structure that starts from one fact—serious as a crime—to arrive at another with no relation to the first, except that it's illuminated by the selfsame light.

The dangerous thread
of things

WHAT I don't know when I'm asked how a film is born is precisely how the birth itself—the delivery, the "big bang," the first three minutes—takes place. And whether the images of those first three minutes have an inner life of their own. In other words, whether a film originates as a response to an inner need of its author or whether the question asked by those images is destined to be nothing more than a question, to have value— ontologically—for what it is.

Let me give you an example.

I wake up one morning with some images in my head. I don't know where they come from, how, or why. In succeeding days and months they recur, and I can't keep them from coming, I can't even get rid of them. I go on looking at them, and I make mental notes which I later jot down in a notebook.

I transcribe them here, with indications of the different places and moments in which this idea of a film was born.

Rome. May 22nd, 1977, 5:30 P.M.
A woman with a stalk of cane in her hand, on a beach in the south. I have no reason for saying it's a southern beach, but this is something I know. With the cane the woman traces a line as yellow as the cane itself. The woman's wearing a white blouse and a brownish skirt, black shoes with high heels, a very long

white scarf at her neck, her dark hair tied at the nape. I don't succeed in defining the color of the scarf, but I note that it's transparent like her blouse. I infer that the woman has no inhibitions and she's very beautiful.

A colorless day is in the making. The sea is calm, glassy.

Paris. The same day, 9:25 P.M.
The woman turns repeatedly backward, to right, to left, without the slightest curiosity.

The beach ends at a promontory covered with shrubs and wild plants, extremely steep. Only when she looks in that direction does the woman show a certain apprehensiveness. The reason for this apprehensiveness is a violet stain there in front of me that slips away whenever I think I've caught it.

Paris. May 27th, 6:00 A.M.
A pathway covered with sand or dust leading to the beach. It's very steep. Two horses come down the path, slipping down side by side, digging in their hooves and raising a huge cloud of dust.

Out of the dust appears a girl.

The girl goes up the path and meets the horses coming down. She passes between the two animals as though she hadn't seen them. She gazes intensely ahead of herself, at something or someone.

But there's no one up there, there's nothing there. Only the wind. It's the wind, not the horses, raising the dust. The horses have disappeared.

Khiva (Uzbekistan). June 26th, 6:45 A.M.
The sky is transparent and gives the feeling that from one moment to the next you can see beyond, see the infinite. The sky is one color. The infinite is another color that we don't know.

One fact suddenly becomes clear to me: the two horses belong to the girl's father. They're two old horses. They were colts when she was a little girl. Now they're twelve, she's eighteen. Her father was sixty-nine, her mother fifty, when she was conceived. She feels she's a monster.

Kokand (Tagikistan). May 28th, 4:30 P.M.
I don't know what the connection is between the girl and the woman. They reappeared to me side by side, the girl's pink darkened by the woman's brown. They move slowly forward, the woman one step ahead of the girl. Always together. Close but not touching. An important fact. They're two individual people, not to be confounded, and the little space always between them suggests the amorous space in which they move, extremely narrow.

Maybe they love each other. Or maybe they think they love each other but it's not true. But for whom isn't it true if there are no witnesses of their feelings?

Melbourne. July 9th, 2:45 P.M.
Again, the woman's on the beach with the girl. Both of them look as though they were at home in this place. They spend a large part of the day here.

I seem to recall (it's a piece of information with the savor of a memory) that the girl had a sister a few years older than she and that, given the very advanced age of her parents, this sister was her whole domestic world. When she died, the girl was overcome by such a great feeling of loneliness, inward emptiness, and even loss—as though a part of her had been taken away—that she set about finding somebody who could take her place, on whom she could discharge the burden of her affections.

Now she thinks she's met her, this person. She likes the bond, clean and clear, that's developed between them.

Sidney. July 13th, 10:00 P.M.
It's not true that the relationship is clean and clear. The girl has the revelation one evening when she sees the woman at the foot of her bed gazing intently at her with heavy eyes.

Nothing indicates whether the house is hers or the woman's.

No furniture but a bed. A window opens in front of the bed. Outside the window can be seen a fire on the beach and the horses come and go, shining with reflections from the fire.

Once when they were colts they used to gallop, running wild, over this sand.

The woman says something to the girl, I hear the voice, not the words. But there's nothing incomprehensible in that sound. This is the idea, and it was suggested to me by a remark in Faulkner's *Sartoris*—"If you have the bad luck to fall in love, I'll kill the man."

Paris.   *October 18th, 5:30 A.M.*

The girl's with a man. I don't know how much time has passed, but it's not important. The man's talking, he gestures with both hands and little movements of his head. From the way the girl waits to hear, it's clear she's greatly interested in his words, she's greatly interested in him. She looks at him the way she looks at the sea, with the same enchanted gaze.

Paris.   *Same day, 9:00 A.M.*

It's morning and I'm thinking of this glimmer of a story while outside it's snowing. I say I'm thinking because this time it wasn't spontaneous images that took me back to the plot. I willed it myself. I suddenly noticed that the unconsciousness with which the film was coming into being would never amount to anything unless I impose limits. In other words, the moment's come to organize the ideas and only the ideas. To transform all this instinctive material into reflective substance. To think of the subject in terms of articulating the scenes, of beginning, development, and end, in short, of structure. It's necessary for the image-making to become intelligible (I was about to say "edible"); you have to help it provide itself with a meaning. Roland Barthes says that a work's meaning can't be created on its own, that the author can produce only conjectures of meaning, of forms if you like, and it's the world that fills them.

But how can Barthes rely on so uncertain an entity as the world?

With these thoughts in my head I look at the snow coming down on the roofs and I'm tempted (more than a temptation, it's a curiosity to verify what happens visually) to make it fall on the beach and the horses also, and to put the two female characters together at the window to look at the sight, in an atmosphere of easy surrender, or uneasiness, or anguish.

The man's appearance could take place in a second reel. I'm dealing probably with a mature man, a man who no longer has the patience and unconsciousness that love requires, who no longer has the language of love.

The woman's position is different. She expects nothing where the girl's concerned. She observes in her a resistance not so much physiological as psychological and then resolves to assist her, to do her pleasure, and if this pleasure is one with the man's, so much the worse. Or so much the better. So long as they don't exclude her. She'd threatened to kill him, but it's too obvious that at the point they've reached it would be a sure way of putting an end to the affair. And although she has a mature capacity for endurance, she couldn't endure that.

And the girl? The girl is freer of preconceptions but it's also she who least perceives the dangerous thread of the affair in which they're getting entangled. For her the woman and the man are only places, like that house and the beach with its horses symbolic of her childhood, in which to live, fulfill herself emotionally and sexually.

Paris. Same day, 1:00 P.M.

I go again to the window. The piercing cold makes the wholly white landscape more vivid. And it's from this whiteness that I get the feeling of finding myself looking at a blank page on which to begin writing again, or rather of a huge screen to be filled.

Whiteness is a color-shadow, it's been said. And while I pass hurriedly over this consideration (which is Rudolf Steiner's), sud-

denly a thick shadow settles down on the events imagined up to
this point. Its entanglements, its twistings, its forcings fuse and
fuse again, then dissolve. What remains is a flat, linear story,
the story of two women who at different times have loved the
same man. Chance makes them meet and talk of this man, who
in this way becomes the cause of their bond, no less profound
than that which they had with him. No retrospective jealousy.
Only friendship. The most limpid and most problematic of all
sentiments.

This is the subject I wrote. Jotted down in a notebook a few
months later, on my return from Khiva, it remained there, forgotten in a little hotel of which I remember the wide corridors
and the filthy toilets.

The odd thing is that this subject, born years ago, is ideally
situated after another written later and that it's embedded in the
film I'm about to start shooting. In fact, it's the sequel to it. All
of which implies that, if it's only cause and effect that set this
event after the other in my mind, then it's necessary to acknowledge in mental events the same movements and mechanisms
that coordinate (or disconnect) the real events of our lives.

Who is the third? . . .

WHEN I've finished a film, it's always with great effort that I start thinking of another. But it's the only thing left for me to do, and which I know how to do. Sometimes I linger over a verse I've read, the poem for me is extremely moving:

Who is the third who walks always beside you?[13]

When a line of poetry becomes a feeling, it's not difficult to put it into a film. This line of Eliot has often tempted me. He gives me no peace, that third who walks always beside you.

In the cup of a lily

To breathe in the cup of a lily . . .

I don't recall who wrote this other line of verse, but the first time I read it, it found its way into a letter written many years back, a letter which could be part of an epistolary film.

I should say what I mean by epistolary film, but that would be a technical discussion and out of place. I allude merely to the potential cinema has for sharpening our sense of the absent interlocutor, that is, the recipient of the letter, by showing him or listening to him.[14]

With an air of total self-confession, the woman who writes what follows is thinking of the man, of his possible reactions, of his eventual response. She's provoking him. Behind her words there's more of him than her. I mean that, for the length of the letter, I'd hold, my camera fixed on the recipient at least as much as the writer. To feel the collision of their voices.

Dearest,

You come to see me on Sundays and that's where my week ends. Now I tell you that we can't go on like this, painfully ending the week this way and then starting all over on Monday. I feel I'm falling to pieces, and I no longer believe in it. What's to be done? Do you think there's anything to be done? Yesterday I went to bed early. I wanted to weep over myself, to think, to free myself. I didn't sleep a wink. I've never seen how a room spends the night. There was a lily on the table and the room was bathed in its perfume. In the cup of the lily there's a shadow that makes the flower more white. I put my mouth into that shadow and breathed until I almost fainted. I went to sleep this morning, which is Monday.

The wheel

A married man, with no children, has had a mistress for two years. His wife knows about it. She's repeatedly asked him to put a stop to this ambiguous sort of life. The man has promised to do so, he's asked her to be patient.

"You'll see, it'll be over. You know the sort of man I am."

For two years. He's a thin man, forty or so, extremely expressive but slow in his movements, out of laziness. Her name is Patrizia. Clear complexion, bright eyes, tapering hands. Naturally restless. Now more than ever. She's reached the point at which she can no longer put up with her husband's affair, and one night she tackles him.

"It's her or me."

And since her husband is once again incapable of deciding, she leaves. For the time being, she goes to a hotel. He accompanies her himself.

Leaving the hotel, Roberto is very depressed. He doesn't know what to think of himself. He doesn't know how to spend the first hours of that unexpected loneliness. He needs to free himself from the sense of guilt he obscurely feels. And the bitterness that his wife's night-time move to the hotel has produced in him. He's had precious little joy from his whole married life. He'd like to tell someone about it, but he can't think of anyone who's available at that time of night. His mistress maybe. As an interested party she's the least appropriate person, but he has no choice.

First, the minute he gets there he finds himself in the sweet-ness of those sleepy naked arms, and they make love. Olga's a girl with two happy eyes and a perfect nose. Everything in her seems perfect, starting with her character and a mysterious qual-ity of hers that makes her always be where you think she is. If you're looking for her somewhere, there she is. One of those women whose very existence gives pleasure.

Roberto tells her everything. Olga raises her hands in a gesture that seems to say, What can I do about it? But the gesture is followed by a few tears running slowly down her face. She rejects this role he and his wife now assign her. She's ready to move aside, to give him up and, if necessary, disappear from his life. She detests making people suffer. While telling him, she gets red in the face, her eyes shine. It's the very emotion that irritates her and that's most like her.

"If you leave," Roberto tells her, looking at her all over, "you'll make me suffer."

But the next morning when, for the first time in his married life, he wakes up alone, the day's tension no longer sustains him and a heavy sadness comes over him. He has a lot to do that day. Badly or well, he does it. Toward evening he goes to his wife's hotel. He finds her with a mutual woman friend of theirs, both drunk. He's seen her drunk on other occasions, it's one of their stupid habits, a periodic celebration of their personal in-dependence.

"Can I keep you company?" he'd once asked them.

"Where do you fit in?" was the answer. "If we're not alone, what independence do we have?"

Patrizia's sitting on the toilet where she's just vomited. A heavy stench assails Roberto. Her friend is on the floor in the half-lotus position holding a glass in her hand as if it were a flower. When she sees him come in, she gets up and disappears. Patrizia starts talking with that slurred speech typical of drunks: "You know . . . you know I've never been twenty? I was eighteen when I married you and now look at me, I'm thirty and I'm alone."

She's distraught. She throws her arms around his neck, sob-bing.

"Don't leave me . . . don't leave me!"

The same whisper with which she once said, "I love you." And he, as he once did, holds her, feeling clearly that nothing is any longer what it used to be. The feeling of intelligence he'd once found living close to her isn't there any more. Now it's a question of conscience. And also of calming her down, promising her he won't leave. If she'd just go back home.

Patrizia pulls back as if she'd been rejected. She'll never go home until he leaves that woman. What makes him say that it's alright, that he'll do what she wants, is a mystery to her. She has no regrets, no nostalgia for reviving a dead romance, needless to say. Maybe he's saying Yes because for him the woman's dead, and the wishes of the dead should be respected. Or maybe it's only his need to finish the big scene when he doesn't have the lines. She concludes that she's going right away to tell everything, she'll tell everything, to Olga.

She's on her way when her girlfriend meets her. All she has to do is look her in the face, take note of her silence, to understand how much has happened.

"Don't be silly, you're not solving anything," she tells him softly. Roberto's only reply is to bend down and kiss her. Every so often it happens that way with them. They kiss and that's the end of it.

His parents are waiting for him under a tree at the door of his apartment. Roberto is forced to invent an excuse to explain his wife's absence. His parents are very fond of Patrizia, at least in words. Actually it's as though she didn't exist. He, their son, their own flesh and blood—he exists. His mother is a woman who bustles about a great deal, who loves meddling with others, who's always agitated. His father, however, isn't interested in anyone and he's serene. He fills this serenity by talking. One placates him by listening. But Roberto has too much to think about to endure the pointless futility of his father's conversation.

"Mother, why don't you murder him?" he says, moving toward the door.

Fifteen minutes later he's at Olga's. The girl gives the impression of being at home waiting for him. Tender, pretty, as much

in love as ever. It doesn't even enter Roberto's mind to tell her
how much he had resolved, how much he'd promised Patrizia,
to tell her. Their conversation even takes a turn in the opposite
direction. They talk openly about getting married, in Mexico
maybe, with a honeymoon trip thrown in. They remain together
all night in an atmosphere of thoughtlessness in which, without
being aware of it, they put a certain solicitude.

Time passes. Their intention of getting married grows stronger.
Roberto sees Olga every day, several evenings in a restaurant.
In one of these restaurants he runs into Patrizia with a group of
dreary people. His wife gives him an amused nod by way of
greeting, and he responds hastily so as not to show the hurt he
feels. He leaves the restaurant and takes Olga to another one,
but the evening's wrecked. Also because Olga makes a mistake.
It's Robert's name-day and at the table the girl takes a package
from her purse and gives it to him. A present. Roberto keeps
turning the package over in his hands. They've been together
for a year and a like occasion has never occurred. Olga doesn't
know he doesn't like receiving presents or being feted on his
name-day, that he doesn't like saying thank you. In fact, Roberto
puts the package in his pocket without opening it. He thinks of
Patrizia who has her own theory on the psychology of presents.
 The next day he goes to find her. He goes there thinking that
she's resentful of his behavior at the restaurant, but she's calm,
overtly distant. He points it out. She starts laughing.
 "If you find me distant it means you're viewing me from a
distance."
 The fact is that she's trying to distance him because she's
certain that's what he wants.

I've often thought of the absurdity of our emotional and psychological situations. What's more, of the absurdity of building
and living in *these* houses and loving *like this*, on one of these
gigantic (but with respect to what?) spheres suspended in space.
The temptation to evade this stupidity by giving a new thrust to

Roberto's character is strong, but the story I'm telling runs on rails that go back a long ways, to the years of *La notte*, to which in some way it has to be a sequel. To push it in a different direction is to risk derailing it.

So Roberto has an instant of perplexity. All he has to do is reach out a hand and seize the propitious moment offered to him and the long parenthesis called Patrizia would be over. He doesn't make this gesture. He does the opposite. He tells his wife the affair with the mistress is over. She stands there looking skeptically at him.

"We'll see," she murmurs.

Roberto turns the corner: "Would you do me a favor? Telephone my mother that it's been a while since she's seen you."

Somewhat reluctantly Patrizia calls. Her mother-in-law wants to see her right away, she has a lot to do but she's expecting her, she's expecting them right away at the house. Patrizia tries to avoid the pain of this meeting, but the other insists so strongly that they're forced to go. And while his mother's in the bedroom with her daughter-in-law, Roberto's with his father who starts talking and talking while Roberto listens, feeling himself sinking into that whirlpool of clichés where the meaning of the words gradually vanishes. But not the voice. It's hard for a voice to become part of us like a sound, the sounds of the sea, for instance, which ends up by becoming inaudible. You can't *not* listen to a voice. And Roberto thinks he'll go mad.

When they reach the street, he's exhausted. Even Patrizia's presence weighs on him at this moment. He needs to be alone. Neither Patrizia nor Olga. Alone. Recover his sense of reality and of himself.

As though intuiting his thoughts, Patrizia moves a few steps away from him.

"Listen . . . ," she says. "Stay with her, listen to me. Let me go. I'll take care of myself."

"But I don't want you to take care of yourself. I want . . . I want to see you smile."

He hands her money, lots of money, and Patrizia smiles without knowing why.

Walking back home, it's as though he'd suddenly lost his sight. His eyes go dark, his head is full of darkness, and this darkness emanates from him to everything outside him. But he has no trouble understanding that the darkness is really inside him, and it's there that his gaze is turned, on that conscience of his that's anything but quiet. It was dishonest on his part to give Patrizia hope, to lie to his parents, to promise to marry Olga. And yet he feels that a sort of sincerity has impelled him to do it. In his own way he's been honest with them all. He's done what they were expecting of him. He's lied only to himself.

This conclusion calms him a little but it doesn't last long. Only as long as it takes him to recall reading in a book a phrase that once seemed mysterious to him, but now no longer does: "Everything's possible, everything but sincerity."

That night he's with his mistress again. He was expecting to spend a few quiet hours with her, those hours that make life a pleasure, when he's suddenly confronted with a new event. Olga's leaving. She has to go to her family's place, a village on the Adriatic coast. She's gone there other times, sometimes with him, but suddenly Roberto's forgotten those times. This departure is something new. In some way it's *the* departure. When Olga tells him, Roberto lowers his eyes to look at his watch. He needs a notion of time. Then he turns his eyes to the girl.

"You're doing it on purpose," he says.

Olga smiles at him sweetly. And, still smiling, she lets herself be embraced and kissed the next day before getting on the train. Out of shame Roberto doesn't stay to watch the train pull out. For the same reason he doesn't telephone her that night. He does so the next morning. Olga's gone out. No reason to be nervous about that. He'll hear from her as soon as she gets back. But he doesn't hear from Olga. He tries to call in the afternoon, he tries again several more times during the night. He can't sleep if he doesn't talk to her. And he doesn't talk to her, he doesn't sleep.

When he gets there, the place is still immersed in the early morning stillness. It's one of those places one sees too often in Italy, places that don't seem to be in Italy. For somebody who's traveled the world, it's an anonymous place.
Roberto's in no hurry. It's too early to go to Olga's, and now that he's a stone's throw away he lets indolence take over. He sits down at a table on the terrace of a bar perched on a pier, orders a cappuccino, and meanwhile writes a postcard to his wife. While sipping the cappuccino, he looks at the landscape.
The sea at that point washes a stretch of shore—palm trees, a beach of fine white sand, shrubs here and there. The sand filters gently into the sea without losing its whiteness since the water is transparent. On one side houses poke up between the pines, on the other there's an odd rocky peak which reveals how the bottom of the sea must look. No volcanic formations here, only shapes formed by erosion, rocky formations of who knows what sort, and oil. Offshore in fact he sees one of the familiar floating oil depots. In some prehistoric era, Middle Eocene let's say, a submovement of the earth had trapped, in any number of underground basins formed here and there throughout the globe, an enormous quantity of fish, billions and billions of fish, making the water ferment, transforming it into oil. But beneath the pier, the sea is still sea, even though it's so still it looks like a lake. You can see very green seaweed, flat as the water, flat like everything else.
It's a landscape in a state of rest.

There was an emergency landing during *Zabriskie Point*, while we were shooting the sequence with that plane that dives within a few feet of the ground in order to buzz the car the girl's driving. It was a small plane with fixed landing-gear, and we were using it for the first time. Our usual plane was a much more maneuverable Cessna 177 with retractable landing wheels. Maybe the pilot thought he was flying the Cessna or miscalculated. The fact is that we hit the roof of the car, demolishing it and seriously injuring one of my assistants who was in the car along with the actress. The collision was very slight. I turned to look down and saw a wheel flying beside the car, and I immediately asked Jim, the pilot, how in the world we'd managaed to knock a wheel off the car when we'd hit the roof.

"It isn't the car wheel," Jim answered, "it's ours. The front wheel."

So our landing gear was minus a wheel. That meant an emergency landing. The dangers were overturning, burning, exploding. There were three of us on the plane, my director of photography, the pilot, and myself. The first went pale and silent. The second was engaged in looking at my assistant lying on the ground like a corpse, and Jim thought he was dead and was overwhelmed, his career as a civil pilot finished, and so on. He was smoking one cigarette after another, brushing his hair, making unthinking gestures—I think he was steering with his feet. He was an exceptional pilot.

But I was calm. I don't know why I was, I had no reason to be. I'd asked Jim a little earlier what our chances were.

"Fifty-fifty" was his reply.

But I was calm. So calm I started throwing out everything that was no longer of any use (everything but the camera) in order to lighten the plane. I even opened the doors, ready to jump. For an hour we circled around the landing strip of that tiny airport in Death Valley. We had to use up our gas and wait for the ambulance, the doctor, the fire engines, and who knows what else. I saw my collaborators and technicians and workmen gathering on the edge of the last stretch of the landing strip to assist our attempt to land. Many had climbed onto the roofs of the cars. I noticed that nobody was getting ready to take pictures.

At the same time I was looking at the surrounding landscape. I was very well acquainted with it, I saw it every day and there was nothing different. And I thought that since it was the same as always there was no reason that we, on the other hand, had to change and go from being alive to being dead. This very natural incredulity even made me smile. Everything was in fact what it was on other days in the same landscape, all but one thing, the tiny wheel that was attached to us before and now wasn't there.

Roberto's calm too, and he's looking at a landscape he knows. Which has the same solid intensity of life as when he saw it other times, the same things. All but one, a little wheel that's no longer there now. The only difference is that Roberto doesn't know it. Thousands of people are waking up in those houses to start their day. Only one is missing. An automobile accident has taken her life.

When Roberto goes to her house, they tell him to go to the hospital. Here he finds her father, an energetic, youthful man. It seems that he wasn't hurt in the accident, but a friend was, and it's his duty to be concerned. Olga died yesterday, tonight they're placing her body in a shiny casket. Just when the grave-diggers are putting in the last screws, Roberto feels choked by an irrepressible emotion, a great emptiness. There it is, the grief is an emptiness that can never be filled again. He makes an effort, he manages not to cry. From that moment a frightful feeling of barrenness possesses him.

He goes back to the city that same night. At home he finds a note from Patrizia asking him to come and see her immediately. What does Patrizia want? With two fingers he lifts the note up against the light in order to see the few lines written on the heavy-weight watermarked paper, then tears it into little pieces. A moment later he opens his fingers. The pieces of paper flutter slowly down and touch the floor without a sound.

Three days

I remember the green meadow, the reddish house, the paving of sun-baked bricks in the midst of the grass. The girl, too, was full of sun. A sun as Nordic as she. I'd never seen her before, she smiled at me with great naturalness and I smiled too but suddenly stopped to ask her if she'd like to come live with me. A profound amazement shone on her face. But not so profound as the point-blank question justified.

Then she came to live with me. It lasted three days. And they were three days of profound amazement.

A film to be made
(or not made)

ONE day I stop my car on a road leading to the pine forest of Ravenna. Sitting in the car, the windows open in order to see better, I look at the long deserted aisles of planted trees in the white, opaque winter light. A geometric labyrinth topped by brown pines. From the paths leading to the beach comes the bright light of the sea. And this is when a situation, a dialogue, enters my thoughts. The characters are a man and a woman— Aldo and Ivana, let's say. He's thirty-nine or so, she's twenty-nine. Dark-haired, both of them. Pale. With this difference, that in him the pallow clashes, in her it confers a certain antique quality, that is, something precious. Aldo's the first to speak.

"I don't recognize a thing any more. There used to be a pine grove here. We went hunting here in the fall. There were sand paths, all twisting. Now these straight aisles confuse me."

"And you, what do you want to do with the site?"

"Me? Nothing. I buy, then sell. For a quarter of a million lire they can do what they want."

"There'll be aisles of trees like this one?"

"I think so."

"Why?"

"What do you mean, why? Because people have a right to get to the sea, and they need houses, trees."

"You like these aisles?"

"No."

"You liked it better the way it used to be?"

"Yes."

"Do you really care whether people can get to the sea?"

Aldo doesn't answer. He lights a cigarette but after two puffs throws it away. Ivana persists.

"I don't understand. You lose something you like in order to do something you don't like, for people you don't know and you aren't even sure it's right for them to have access to the water."

"Don't be silly. Progress, the brotherhood of man, do you understand these things or don't you? Besides, it's a business deal like any other."

"But do you need the money you'll be getting out of it?"

"No."

"You see, it makes no sense."

"Let's go eat instead. You know a place?"

Ivana looks at him with an ironic and combative expression: "Even you know where it is. Follow your nose, you'll get there even if you don't recognize a thing."

The Tagliata is a drainage canal in the reclamation project, with a mold of cinnabar-green on the still water. On the canal, the trattoria-bar. A half hour later Aldo and Ivana are inside that hunters' hangout, old, smoky, and rustic, the sort of place that's now disappeared. They sit down at a table and the dialogue continues. The owner comes up and sits down with them, shoving the chair with his foot.

"Look who's here!"

"Everything's changed. I spent a half hour trying to find your canal."

"Yeah, everything's changed. Even you, driving up in a Mercedes. Hi, Ivana. I didn't recognize you. You know that our little friend here couldn't hit a heifer's ass with a Browning that even in the old days cost a hundred thousand lire?"

"Of course I know it. We were engaged."

"That's right. By the way, how come you . . . ?"

Ivana doesn't answer. The proprietor changes his reserve for a look of sympathy. He's a man as rustic as his trattoria. His eyes have the clarity of swamp water.

"Cheers, what'll we have to eat?"

"What do you have?" Aldo asks.

"Two fat woodcock on the spit."

"No, God, no!"

Ivana shudders. The proprietor laughs and caresses her cheek.

"Forgive me, I forgot. Maybe a chicken, provided you don't know what it is."

Even Ivana laughs. A tacit complicity between the two of them, cheerful and tender. An old joke. Aldo observes them with a twinge of jealousy, feeling left out. The proprietor leaves.

"What's this business with the chicken?" Also asks.

"Nothing. He knows I can't eat birds. The little tiny ones. You can see the claws, the beak. How they're made, I mean."

"It hurts you, I know. All women are the same. Pity and tenderness for the poor little birdies. not for the poor baby cows. Not for old goats with beards. It's a feeling of pity I don't understand."

"I didn't make myself clear. I meant that I don't like them as creatures, these birds. Creatures with wings. Everything with wings. They frighten me, they horrify me."

"You mean you don't love them? Because if you loved them, if they made you feel fond of them, then you'd eat them, no?"

"Yes, in that case . . . At least I think so."

"For instance?"

"Cats."

"Kittens."

"Yes, kittens."

"Soft, playful, independent . . ."

"Like that, yes, I'd eat them."

"For instance . . .me."[15]

Ivana turns to look at him with a quiet open smile: "If I loved you, Aldo."

Other dialogues

SOMETIMES I stop to listen to two people talking. Their conversations are often so attached to the faces that utter them that it comes naturally to me to develop an idea about them. My ideas are almost always ideas about films. The plots emerge spontaneously from faces like those.

1.

—What are you doing in these parts?

—There's a piece of land I want to buy.

—How's Giulia?

—Not well.

—Where's the property?

—Behind the church, about a mile. Why don't you go and see her? She's very sick. It'll please her.

—Sure, I'll go. How many acres?

—Fifty. Development property.

—Price?

—If you go see her, tell her I'm close, despite everything. Fifteen million, two hundred thousand lire.

—It's a good price. I'll let her know.

Both men are silent. They seem to be reflecting. About Giulia? About the property?

II.

—What's wrong with you?

—Let me handle it. I've gotten him to 110 million lire, but he ought to make another offer. Higher, higher.

—How high can he go, do you think? I mean, what's the piece of land worth?

—I told you, 110 million.

—And we've already reached that figure. But tell me, that piece of land, in that site, with all those trees, it must somehow have an intrinsic value.

—It does, the minute a buyer shows up. And then you've got to see. For someone who wants to build a villa there, let's say, and spend all his life because he likes being there, etc., it's priceless.

—Alright. But for someone who wants to build?

—A speculation, you mean?

—Yes.

—A camping ground, for instance, or whatever . . . ?

—That's it, someone who wants to put in a camping ground here.

—Hmm, depends.

—Depends on what?

—It's one thing if the deal's been closed and set and there's hard cash on hand. Another thing if . . .

—But do you want to sell or not?

—But why ask me?

—Because you're the broker. In short, how much would *you* pay?

—I don't have a lira.

—But if you did, if you had all the capital you wanted?

—You mean my own personal capital or a bank loan?

Etcetera.

Just for staying together

A man and a woman in a seaside restaurant. Sparkling red wine, homemade bread and salami. The salami's the color of the wine, that's why, the only reason why, they're drinking it.

A dog comes up and approaches the table where the man and woman are sitting. He looks around, sees the proprietress, knows she doesn't like to see him nosing around among the customers, and turns back toward the door. Here he stops. The proprietress goes to the kitchen and the dog returns. He knows all he has to do is pretend he's obedient.

Gradually the two get drunk. They've decided to get drunk. The half-empty room, the proprietress, the dog, even the sea disappear. The world's a tablecloth, three feet by three feet. The world's white. They don't even need to say certain things. They talk about steaks, tagliatelle, about everything they haven't eaten, and about three men who've just come in, two fat men and one skinny one. They talk about their hands, about the position of their hands on the tablecloth, that is, on the world.

But now they've got to get moving, resume their journey.

On the point of going out, they hesitate. They have the feeling they'll never manage to get through the door. In fact the woman totters, laughs, and collapses onto a chair. The dog watches her. You can't make a fool of yourself in front of the dog, says the man.

Outside now it's raining. A gentle drizzle which a breeze scatters here and there. The woman leans her head on the wet roof of the car. She remains like that for several minutes. A heavy grayness in the form of a cloud seems to be stuck to her back. When she looks up, the man notices that she's crying. Or laughing. Or crying and laughing at the same time. Their stories come out without even speaking. The man also begins laughing, but his eyes are moist. These damnable identities of their characters, two incompatible identities that make their relationship impossible. They're a man and a woman pointlessly made for each other.

A voice cries out:

"Vera!—and the name is followed by a curse. The man and the woman look at each other. The woman stops crying or laughing and with a very feminine movement gets into the car. The man watches her and then gets in himself. He feels virile and clear-headed. He starts the car and steps on the gas. The car drives off with a roar, leaving wheel tracks on the wet paving.

The dog's come to the door to watch them.

This was the beginning of a film. Rather it was the whole film. My conjecture was to concentrate the action on that hour and a half the meal lasted. In that atmosphere of tense euphoria. A film with a beginning and maybe no end.

I've always wondered whether it's always right to provide an ending for stories, whether literary, theatrical, or cinematic. Once it's been firmly channelized a story's in danger of dying inwardly unless you give it another dimension, unless you let its tempo prolong itself in that external world where we, the protagonists of all stories, live. Where nothing's conclusive.

"Give me new endings," said Chekhov once, "and I will reinvent literature."

From a thirty-seventh floor over Central Park

Soundtrack for a film in New York

THERE'S a continuous background noise, dull and low: traffic. And another less continuous sound, the wind. It comes in gusts but in the pauses I hear it blowing against other skyscrapers in the distance. Each gust is followed by a swaying of the skyscraper up at the top where I am, and I notice a curious sensation, as though for a few instants my brain had stopped perceiving.

On and off, a short weak siren. Two honks of a horn. A roar moving away, then coming closer, is erased by a sudden, impatient gust. A bus.

It's 6 A.M.

A second roar combines with the first, overwhelms it. A barely audible explosion, very far away. The wind returns, rising from nothing, expands, seems to spread in the still air, but stops instead. Again a hint of a bus. It isn't a bus, it finally reveals itself, a car. This second sound could be a motorcycle, but it suddenly becomes a different sound, what I don't know. A truck, a second truck accelerating. Two or three cars passing, exhaust pipes stuck there like an organ, bursts fading skillfully away. An instant of absolute emptiness, frightening. A truck very close, almost as if it were on the second floor. But it immediately fades. A shriek. A boat siren, long and melancholy. The wind's died. The siren continues. Noise in the background, beneath the siren. A bell ringing, fuzzily, garbled. Like a country church. But maybe it's something hitting on iron, not a bell. Another. Two. Angry intrusion of a car's engine accelerating, very brief. In an unexpected silence, the siren continues in the distance. That echo of metallic sound comes forward. A very noisy truck seems to be climbing toward the window. But it's an airplane. All the noises grow stronger—horn, siren, truck—then gradually attenuate. But no, another roar, then again the shrillilng of the siren. Irritating but suggestive, it makes you sense the horizon.

6:15.

All the preceding sounds are there, lined up in a row as in a sample-book, distinct. Brief parenthesis. The background noise is still there and, always, the siren. A sharp honk of a horn, very far away. Another here below, discreet. A car on a faraway street, very fast, probably European. The wind slaps several times against the wall outside my building; a single gust immediately drowned out by the usual truck sound, but more moaning this time, followed by a second one, but a compact, a new motor, its distinct knockings sliding away, fusing with each other. But it's not a truck, it's a second airplane. No, it's not a plane, it's a sound arrogantly growing and suddenly dying without declaring itself. The siren still sounding, obsessive, together with somebody whistling (how can that be?), suddenly interrupted by a furious honking. Sound of planks falling on top of other planks. Very distinct: a pulley, the clacking of the cogs. But it can't be a pulley, and that continuous note can't be a siren. More planks, with something metallic added. It's a dull, barely audible sound, but it still leaves an echo in the air. A sort of timid musical note which suddenly stops. Cars passing, one, a second, a third, on and on and on . . . They cross with other cars, different sounds. A plane that seems to have emerged from inside a skyscraper. It disappears as unexpectedly as it appeared. A splendid roar of a car, just right for that moment. It passes and dies, recognizable, satisfying. Two notes, trembling. A gust.

6:30.

More gusts. The wind returns furiously, slipping between the skyscrapers, seems to wriggle out, bursts boldly onto the park. A horn silences it as though it had been slapped. The wind's gone. A ringing, in the silence, and still that siren, a note higher. It wasn't a ringing, it was my Italian ear that defined it that way. The planks: a sharp blow like a volley. A subway train, you'd think it was the old El. Ringings prolonged to a siren wail. Very brief. A hint and it's gone. Sounds have a short life too, they're born and die in a few instants. The background roar becomes organized, moves forward like a camouflaged army, advances *en masse*, ready for anything, or to prevail uncontested. It's very close, you can distinguish wind, cars, plane, a clanking of old iron, and the siren, they advance resolutely on the hotel sky-scraper. At the head now is that sound of clanking iron, but the plane passes it, it's alone now. Nothing. The battle's over. Modest revolution smashed by a honk of authoritarian horn. Bangings on wood. A pause. More bangings. They're moving planks, no doubt about it. It sounds like a machine gun about to break down. It fires on the cars which are forced to stop. A second siren, more real. The sound of a truck's wheels, but it's not a truck, it's the wind picking up again, stronger now but not enough to drown out a plane. Cars. An explosion like a cannon, with no echo. Scattered here and there, metallic sounds disposed on different planes. An angry gust, an angry truck, the angry subway train. Two bursts of different tonality. The roar increases but immediately stops, as though impeded by the resumed bangings. Other distinct sounds that I don't recognize come to life, a long stunning horn that doesn't die, won't ever die, I no longer hear it but it's left this certainty. In contrast the wails of the siren are dying. In fact a gust supresses them, while a truck rises straight up. But it falls back down, confused in the wind. A sort of bell. A voice, the first voice.

7 A.M.

A sudden burst of the siren, as though to remind me that it's still there now, as unnoticed as it is persistent. Squealing tires. A bellowing inside a tunnel.

8:30.

The sun has risen but the noises haven't changed. Only one's been added, an unplesant one: drillers demolishing a building.

They're far away but every now and then, according to the wind, I can make them out. The other sounds are the same. An anxious rhythmical whistle repeating itself as though announcing something, a whistle with narrative ambitions. A noisy car, no, not a car, a machine of what sort I don't know, noisy, and the drillers in the distance. Except that everything's become stronger. The sounds have increased with the light. Likewise the wind, likewise the car motors. Likewise the siren. Only the horns have become scarcer, evidence of people heeding traffic regulations, people who blow their horns only when forced. They don't have money to spend on fines and they're also careful to obey the law, a bit German. I see them, in this confused roar, fused together, the same eyes intent on driving, the same gestures, the same children, inside their slow cars: a roar that lacks the courage to explode. Like an airplane stopped in mid-air, the clean clear air of this spring-like winter.[16]

A morning and an evening

LET'S try thinking of a film that tells the story of two days in a man's life. The day he's born and the day he dies. A life whose prelude seems to start on one road and whose epilogue shows that he's taken a route quite different, even geographically speaking, from where he started.

Let's try thinking of a film with a morning and a night, but not the interim anxieties.

Don't try to find me

THE day Marta leaves isn't a day like all the others. Marta's leaving is a unique and decisive event, one of those that remain forever nailed down in one's memory. As if that weren't enough, it's a stupid day. There's rain and there's sun. You don't see it, you don't know where it is, but the light's there and it's very strong. Even the rain is very strong. A cloudburst of sunlight. The living room windows are open and the sun coming in slides across the floor at the same speed as the clouds, slowly. The rain on the other hand stops at the windowsills.

The thing that strikes him most is the sound of his own footsteps in the half-empty room, a barely perceptible echo that follows him everywhere. At first it wasn't there. At first all the sounds went away like his wife, like the truck with part of the furniture. The sounds went away, the silences arrived.

He's done his best to have as few habits as possible. The habit of sounds he wasn't able to avoid. He began listening as a boy on the day when he imitated the striking of the hour by the clock on a very distant belltower and won a bet. It was a discovery for him too, his exceptional hearing. Which promptly provoked another discovery, the miracle of sounds. Why does a piece of iron striking against another piece of iron emit audible vibrations? And why do these vibrations, once emitted, die away instead of spreading indefinitely through the air? How is the perception of those vibrations translated into sound in our brain? In short,

what is it to *hear*? At school they told him that colors have no
well-defined properties. But sounds do. From that time on his
days were articulated by sounds. Every hour with its own sounds.
Until it became a habit, and then his job. Sitting there at a console
with forty-eight channels, memory bank, synthesizer, and so
forth, immersed all day in those compact, obsessive sonorities
which, in the society of the young, comment on our age.

Even the telephone has a different ring. Almost offensive. It
isn't Marta. It's someone who wants his address, to send
him . . .

"Please, don't send me anything."

And then an hour later, while he's getting out of the bathtub
where he ended up for no reason, another ring. It's her. His first
thought is, where's she calling from? He asks her but she doesn't
want to tell him. His second thought is, "And so where do I go
look for her when she hangs up?"

Marta's arguments on the telephone all focus on one point,
today or tomorrow, what's the difference? They knew it, they'd
told each other so often that this day would come. Did they really
know it? And so? So to hell with it. To know it, that is, vaguely
to think it every so often is one thing, finding yourself faced with
the fact is another. The facts are pitiless, they don't care about
us, our emotions, our pain. Or about his feeling of impotence,
about the collapse of his whole self. That's the odd thing, about
himself, not their relationship.

The telephone call lasted five minutes. And now he's there in
the half-empty room face to face with his whole life, as cold as
though it were somebody else's life.

How in the world is it that he only now remembers the little
boy?

It must have been the silence that brought him to mind, the
absence of his sounds. The shrieks, the desperate wails, the
banging of discarded objects, his clumsy tramping on the floor,
the buzzing of toys that turned into toy carcasses a day later.
And his own name suddenly shouted out for no reason, in a

piercingly loud voice. He'd also learned how to click his tongue
and amused himself immensely doing it, proud of knowing how,
the minute he felt he was being looked at. It was impossible to
waste the day, as he liked doing on holidays, with that confusion.
It was like not wasting it.

He'd never regretted not having children. He'd literally found
him on his hands and he hadn't known what else to do except
start studying him like a textbook, a book he didn't like. Those
whose love children end up by finding something beautiful in
them all. In that clumsy little body, in those movements dictated
by a logic he didn't understand, in those mangled words—"jam-
mies" for "pajamas," "tory" for "story," "eye" for "buy" (he always
made the same mistake, never did "buy" come to mind when
the child was stammering out "I" or "eye," which means "eye"
until there's proof to the contrary, a part of the body, who could
have taught him the word "buy"? Obviously you, only you use
the word "buy" in this house, Marta observed with a laugh)—in
all this he found nothing gracious or endearing, only irritation
and a desolate lack of elegance. But for Marta everything was
what it should be, that is, normal. She behaved and talked to
the child as though he were a grown-up. No affectations, none
of that cooing baby talk that mothers use with children of that
age.

Standing in front of the window, eyes shut, he listens to the
rain stopping and through his eyelids feels the sunlight appear-
ing. Any kind of weather suited Marta. Cloudy, fair, hazy, rainy,
snowy, even those days that are neither one nor the other. Marta's a young woman with an empty past and a future that is
anything but full. A future as a mother left with nothing but
grown-up thoughts. She has no doubts, she asks no questions
and spares herself the nuisance of asking them. Her hopes focus
on her son, nothing else.

That he was also his son he said again and again, while she
listened. One day when he feels the bond of blood is weaker
than ever, he actually shouts it out. But the boy's chaotic and

petulant soundtrack erases his conscience. That tiny being makes his life a cacophony, contradicts it. He's happy enough with the way his adult life is going, running like a river that's reaching flood stage. It's as though this son had checked the current. Suddenly one night this idea comes to him: maybe he's not even related to the boy. It's an absurd idea, but one which, with the rage common to absurdity, becomes a stubborn persuasion. With a meticulousness he himself deems detestable, he sets about confirming his suspicion. He scrutinizes his son. He reviews the years, one by one, to see if their passage has left recognizable signs—signs he regards as his own natural characteristics, his physical traits. Finding not even the shadow of a resemblance, he feels estranged from the boy and loathes him. The boy and the man he will eventually become. Both of them. From that moment he starts avoiding him. In the hours spent at home he forces himself not to think of the boy's presence in the other rooms, mentally confounding it with the noise of the traffic.

Meanwhile, without noticing it, he becomes more attentive and amorous with Marta. And he doesn't understand that the attentions and the love subtracted from his son are also subtracted from her, and she withdraws.

One afternoon she comes home with a truck, loads it with some furniture and two suitcases, and leaves. Without a whisper, almost stealthily. An hour later on the telephone she tells him why. At any other moment he would have known what to answer. But there alone, in that emptiness that returns the echo of his own words, he has nothing to say. And so they're both quiet. Four minutes of dialogue, one of silence. The commemoration *ante litteram* of their farewell.

The film is the story of those five years and these five minutes. It could be titled *Don't Try To Find Me*, her last words on the telephone.[17]

Notes

1. "But even if I do not know how the world originated, nonetheless from the very ways of heaven and from many other facts, I would dare to assert that the world was certainly not created for us by a divine power: so great are the flaws with which it is endowed."

2. An "event horizon" might be termed the "ultimate horizon" of physics—a frontier from which, as in a black hole, no information could in theory escape. The inner energy-producing limit (or ergo-sphere) of a black hole would be the "event horizon." Gravity there is so incredibly powerful that nothing, not even the highest-energy particles or light waves, could escape. A particle moving or falling toward this "event" would seem to cease moving because it had entered an area where gravity had brought time to a standstill; it would disappear into what is jocularly called The Big Crunch.

   Antonioni's interest in cosmology and astronomy is, like that of his observer here, of long standing. In his famous Cannes interview after the screening of *L'avventura*, he commented:

   > Consider Renaissance man, his sense of joy, his fullness, his multifarious activities. These Renaissance men were of great magnitude, technically able and at the same time artistically creative, capable of feeling the Ptolemaic fullness of man. Then man discovered that his world was Copernican, an extremely limited world in an unknown universe. And today a new man is being born, fraught with all the fears and terrors and stammerings that are associated with a period of gestation . . .

   The same cosmological—and indeed post-Copernican—background to the transience and cultural disquiet of gestating modern man is invoked in Antonioni's first feature-length film, *Cronaca di un amore* (1950), where the lovers meet in the Milan planetarium. Against their whispered words is set the voice of the lecturer: "The universe is expanding, through holes in the Milky Way we can glimpse . . ." Antonioni himself asserts that President Kennedy, just before being assassinated, had granted him permission to participate in a space flight. In *La notte* (1961) amateur rocketeers talk of reaching the moon. As originally scripted, *Red Desert* (1964) had a fantasy sequence of a kite whose flight is brushed by rockets being launched from Cape Canaveral. In *Identification of a Woman*, the final shot is another sci-fi fantasy: an object that looks like an asteroid-spaceship hurtling toward its own (and the fantasizing director's) immolation in the sun—or personal "event horizon." So, in the present "nucleus-fiction," the human event horizon—death— parallels the cosmic event horizon in an isotropically receding universe, everything moving toward the infinite or perhaps finite "horizon of horizons."

3. This is the narrative nucleus from which Antonioni is reportedly about to shoot his next film.

4. The phrase comes from the *Life* of St. Teresa, the motto of whose Carmelite order is *Patire o morire* ("To suffer or die"). In *Variety* (October 4, 1978) Antonioni was reported to be at work on a new film based on a religious theme: "The project is entitled 'Suffer or Die' from his own original story and screenplay . . . In an exclusive interview . . . Antonioni said that the film would reflect some of the major existential dilemmas of the individual living in today's terribly difficult society and would fundamentally express the groping of the protagonist toward God—a protagonist who does not believe in God but is moving in that direction." As the narrative nucleus of "This Body of Filth" makes quite clear, it is not Antonioni but his protagonist who is moving in a religious direction. Always and avowedly secular, Antonioni's persistent interest in the idea of transcendence here fixes on the religious dimension of that theme— as it will again in the secular "pilgrimage" and "passion" of Locke in *The Passenger*—his gestating "vocation" for a transcendence which, in an earlier age, would have found a role normalized in traditional established religion, but which now finds none. *Patire o morire* was scripted, but then, for financial reasons, aborted.

5. "To give compassion to the wretched."

6. Fitzgerald is one of the four or five writers by whom Antonioni says he has been most influenced. The indebtedness is clearly acknowledged in *L'avventura*, in which the opening shark scare is modeled on the opening scene of *Tender Is the Night*, just as An-

tonioni's Sandro has obvious affinities with Fitzgerald's Dick Diver. Among the missing Anna's possessions are two books: *Tender Is the Night* and the Bible.

7. This narrative nucleus was scripted under the Title of *The Crew* but later, in 1984, abandoned, once again for lack of funds. The film would have been shot in Miami and San Diego, and off Baja California where, during certain months of the year, the sea is utterly becalmed. As developed, the dominant theme would have been the violence (hence, I suppose, the yacht's name, *Irene*—from the Greek *eirenē*, meaning "peace") and the violence erupting (the Third World against the comfortable technological and metaphysical Faustian assurances of the industrialized West) below decks on the becalmed and helpless *Irene* and its executive American "skipper," so involved, erotically and metaphysically, with *his* "Irene" and the "open water" of the ocean.

8. The film was actually scripted in 1956. Set in the twenties, it was also intended to be shot in color.

9. The great pioneering film (1895) of Louis Lumière, the first cinematic farce and probably the first fictional film ever made.

10. The allusion is to a line from the final chorus of *The Family Reunion*: "We do not like to look out of the same window, and see quite a different landscape." Antonionio admits to a lifelong admiration for the poetry of Eliot, whose work moves him, he says, more than that of any modern poet.

11. A televised version of the famous Monteverdi score directed by Ingmar Bergman, but unseen in this country.

12. The image is a recurrent one in Antonioni's work: in *L'eclisse* (1962) Piero's car is hoisted out of the artificial lake into which it was driven by the drunk who stole it—the headlights still gleaming as the car clears the water. In *Identifizcazione di una donna* (1981) the headlights of the car burn through the enveloping fog as though through water. *Etc.*

13. From *The Waste Land*, V. Eliot's note on the line refers the reader to Shackleton's Antarctic expedition, in which the explorers, utterly exhausted, thought there was a third person—Christ, they assumed—accompanying them. Shackleton himself is either alluding to, or unconsciously recalling, the incident of the disciples at Emmaus.

14. In the final sequence of *La notte* (1961) Antonioni experimented with such an epistolary device, as Lidia (Jeanne Moreau) reads to her husband (Marcello Mastroianni) his own love-letter of years earlier, and the camera explores both her face and his while she

reads. The scene was adversely criticized for being too literary, too uncinematic; but the camera exploration of the tension between the two is visually extremely revealing of their present and past relationship.

15. These lines appear almost verbatim in *Red Desert*; the entire narrative here may well have been part of the original script of that film, set in Ravenna and its outskirts.

16. Antonioni, as this soundtrack sequence suggests, has always wanted to do a film set in New York. But his artistic sense of his given frame—the dimensions of the cinemascope screen, its specifically *mural* proportions—has presumably prevented him from doing so. Asked by an interviewer whether he wouldn't someday do a film in New York—rather than London, Rome, Los Angeles, etc.—he replied, "Only when the screen goes vertical."

17. The title of this nucleus—purposely designed to close the book— is presumably a caveat to the reader. The director has always held that in some sense his films represent an effort to find himself, to know himself.